ESSAYS IN INTERNATIONAL FINANCE

No. 217, April 2000

THE REAL PLAN AND THE EXCHANGE RATE

GUSTAVO H. B. FRANCO

INTERNATIONAL FINANCE SECTION

DEPARTMENT OF ECONOMICS
PRINCETON UNIVERSITY
PRINCETON, NEW JERSEY

INTERNATIONAL FINANCE SECTION
EDITORIAL STAFF

Library of Congress Cataloging-in-Publication Data

Franco, Gustavo Henrique Barroso.
    The Real plan and the exchange rate / Gustavo H.B. Franco.
    p. cm. — (Essays in international finance ; no. 217)
    Includes bibliographical references.
    ISBN 0-88165-124-9
    1. Monetary policy—Brazil. 2. Fiscal policy—Brazil. 3. Devaluation of currency—Brazil. 4. Inflation (Finance)—Brazil. 5. Economic stabilization—Brazil.
I. Title. II. Series.
HG835.F732 2000
339.5'0981—dc21   00-020423
                                                                                      CIP

Printed in the United States of America by Princeton University Printing Services at Princeton, New Jersey

International Standard Serial Number: 0071-142X
International Standard Book Number: 0-88165-124-9
Library of Congress Catalog Card Number: 00-020423

CONTENTS

FIGURES

TABLES

THE REAL PLAN AND THE EXCHANGE RATE

1 Introduction

The Real Plan put an end to Brazilian hyperinflation by combining an innovative monetary-reform scheme with active monetary and exchange-rate policies meant to address the fundamental imbalances thought to be at the root of Brazil's impressive inflation record. Even though it has not been considered an exchange-rate-based program, and despite its very good results, the Real Plan has raised a fair amount of controversy. A good part of this controversy has been about exchange-rate management, which many see as the key reason for both the plan's success and the economy's fragility with respect to external shocks. Indeed, the exchange rate has been at the very core of the complex political economy surrounding the stabilization and reform process in Brazil during the last few years. The precise nature of the structural reforms, always mentioned as crucial to stabilization and the restoration of growth, has seldom been fully defined. In the absence of precise specifications, one gets the impression that the issues pertaining to a redefinition of the development model—Brazil's optimal level of openness, the nature and extent of the state's participation in the economy, extreme inequality—were not very important and that the hyperinflation episode was simply a development crisis unworthy of much deep thought, perhaps the result of outright macroeconomic mismanagement. Some skepticism as to the true relevance of structural reforms may be partly justified by the region's prior attempts to justify policy heterodoxy on the basis of regional uniqueness, especially during the years when the structuralists reigned supreme. This was a long time ago, but it may help explain why a rather nonstructural cure-all

The author wishes to thank the Research Department (Depec) of the Banco Central do Brasil and, in particular, Altamir Lopes and Maria do Socorro da Costa Carvalho for their help with figures and their insights to earlier versions of this essay. Comments and suggestions from other former colleagues in public service, especially from Pedro Malan and Demostenes Madureira de Pinho, were extremely helpful. A seminar presentation at the Pontifícia Universidade Católica do Rio de Janeiro (PUC-RIO) and observations from an anonymous referee also helped to broaden the scope of the essay. Research assistance from Debora Masullo and Joana Simões de Melo Costa is also appreciated. The remaining mistakes are my sole responsibility.

1

prescription, a devaluation, so often appears "at the top of the list of reforms needed" (see William Cline's [1997, p. 395] reading of Rudiger Dornbusch's paper).

Indeed, it is very difficult to minimize either the importance of the heavy structural-reform agenda that Brazil has experienced or the complexity of the problems that it needs to address. Hyperinflation is a rare disease seen in only a dozen or so episodes in human history, almost always in the presence of gigantic dislocations such as wars or revolutions. The fact that Brazil experienced a hyperinflation is not always fully recognized, possibly because the phenomenal extent to which indexation disseminated into the Brazilian economy provided an apparent (although implausible) sensation of normalcy. According to Philip Cagan's (1987) classic definition placing the threshold for a hyperinflation at 50 percent a month, Brazil would have experienced this condition only briefly during 1989–90 and, again, during the month of June 1994.[1] Yet, this small caveat should not imply that Brazil was not in a highly exceptional position. As Leslie Armijo (1996, p. 10) put it: "[In view of] the generally *blasé* attitude of Brazilian elites towards price rises . . . policy discourse in Brazil has sometimes appeared to operate in a world of its own; . . . as long as the economy continues to function (as it manifestly has) there can be no hyperinflation." If one lowers the hyperinflation threshold to a monthly rate of 25 percent, however—a figure Michael Bruno (1993, p. 4) finds more appropriate, and which changes nothing about the nature of the process—one would find that Brazil was in continuous hyperinflation for the seven years prior to July 1994. Moreover, the fact that the 50 percent threshold level was reached only a few times during these years is attributable solely to the government's enforcement of economy-wide price freezes on four occasions after the collapse of the Cruzado Plan late in 1986. In playing with numbers, one can easily miss the point that thresholds are of little importance and that hyperinflation, however defined in quantitative terms, is the expression of a terminal disease or is "the outer, nominal (that is, monetary) manifestation of a deep

[1] According to the most commonly used nationwide consumer-price index (INPC), Brazil's inflation reached 51.3 percent a month in December 1989 and climbed to a peak of 82.2 percent in March 1990. In June 1994, the INPC change was 48.2 percent, barely missing 50 percent. The other most commonly used consumer-price index, the IPC-FIPE (from the Fundação Instituto de Pesquisas Econômicas), for the city of São Paulo, shows a similar profile: 51.8 percent in December 1989; 79.1 percent in March 1990, the worst month; and 50.7 percent in June 1994.

underlying disease in the *real* economy, almost like the high fever of an ailing body" (Bruno, 1993, p. 14).[2]

As most Brazilians came to realize how serious the situation was, disbelief gave way to disillusion: How could this have happened to Brazil, a country that had never experienced hurricanes, earthquakes, or civil wars? What kind of hidden mechanisms had derailed this growth machine, second only to Japan in the twentieth century and once hailed as having mastered peaceful coexistence of development with inflation?[3] How could things have gone so wrong?

With hindsight, Brazilians seem now to understand that the foundations of the once highly praised economic miracle—import substitution, substantial state intervention, and inflationary finance—even though effective in mobilizing resources to an unprecedented extent and in establishing Brazil as the sixth largest industrial economy in the world, produced weaknesses that, over time, not only precluded further advancement but also created imbalances that ultimately led to stagnation and hyperinflation. It would seem that the import-substitution growth model was exhibiting decreasing returns—that, as Paul Krugman (1996, p. 169) once said of the socialist and Asian countries, "economic growth that is based on expansion of inputs, rather than on growth in output per unit of input, is eventually subject to diminishing returns." The hyperinflation condition could very well reflect the pains involved in the exhaustion of the old model, just as stabilization could be the indispensable hallmark of a new one. In this context, the notion of "reforms" has been commonly applied to the highly diversified task of recasting the development model in order to address long-neglected issues such as chronic budget deficits, dependence on inflation, growing social inequalities, stagnant productivity growth, low investment in social overhead, inefficient state enterprises, and regulation. Brazilian optimism notwithstanding, the impatience to resume rapid growth in Brazil has been severely tempered by the generalized perception that

[2] Cagan's original definition establishing the 50 percent threshold dates back to his 1956 contribution to Milton Friedman's benchmark studies on the quantitative theory of money. More recently, in his "hyperinflation" entry in the revised edition of the Palgrave *Dictionary of Economics*, Cagan (1987, p. 704) explicitly recognizes that "there is no well-defined threshold" for a hyperinflation, that the phenomenon is "best described by a listing of cases varying quite a lot," and that it should be defined as an "extremely rapid increase in the price level," something that definitely occurred in Brazil.

[3] See Albert Fishlow (1974) for a complete and critical review of claims that Brazil had discovered a bullet-proof formula for such coexistence.

there are structural weaknesses in the economy. Although inflation has seemed to be well under control—even after the 1999 devaluation—the economy is seen as facing limits to growth. Most observers think that overcoming these limits will involve hard-core reforms and modernization, technological dynamism, human-capital investment, and other structural changes not generally included in stabilization packages and not much affected by the exchange-rate regime. The fact that the post-devaluation landscape looks a lot like the earlier panorama only reinforces this impression.

Over time, and by virtue of these perceptions, the stabilization agenda with respect to so-called "fundamentals" has gradually become indistinguishable from the economic-development agenda, a coalescence that seems only natural in light of international experience. Bruno (1993, p. 272) argues that "the distinction between what constitutes the necessary components of macroeconomic adjustment policy and what is mainly relevant to long term growth becomes blurred the closer one looks at the recent successful reforms in Latin America and even more so in the case of Eastern and Central Europe." Natural as it may seem, however, this "second phase" of the stabilization *cum* reform programs may be lengthy and difficult. According to Dornbusch (1991, pp. 45–46), "countries that have experienced protracted high inflation, financial instability, and payment crises will not find their way back to growth easily. Their economies need to achieve not only fiscal reconstruction by thorough budget balancing but also a far-reaching institutional reconstruction that involves a financial system able to provide effective intermediation and a regulatory and trade regime that helps allocate resources to maximize productivity. . . . Economic reconstruction is *a work of a decade or more*" (emphasis added).

It is against this backdrop, and in consideration of the catalytic role played by the Real Plan in the advancement of the reform process, that one should discuss the individual policy components of the Real Plan. Choices about the exchange rate had to be made in connection with the complex and overlapping agendas of stabilization and reform, not to mention the uncertainties naturally involved in a process of profound economic change occurring under unstable external conditions. "The essential question," according to one International Monetary Fund (IMF) study (Guitián, 1993, p. 71), "can be formulated as a straightforward choice between achieving a *nominal* objective, namely, price stability, or meeting a *real* objective, competitiveness. The complexity lies in the difficulty of using economic policy in general, and exchange-rate policy in particular, to attain these goals simultaneously.

4

Though complex, the issue is nothing more . . . than a new version of the age-old conflict between internal and external balance that was discussed in the literature many years back."

Like many (possibly all) other stabilization plans, the Real Plan started, in July 1994, with some appreciation, especially during its first four months, when the currency was allowed to float. The strengthening of the newborn currency was regarded as a sign of confidence in the new stabilization effort and, indeed, played a crucial role in the fight against hyperinflation. Discussions were heated, however, about whether Brazil had a new equilibrium exchange rate (or a significant undervaluation before stabilization) or whether it had an overvalued and unsustainable exchange rate that would need correction at some point in the future. The Brazilian authorities tried to be prudent in the face of these claims, first, by avoiding insurmountable commitments (such as the commitment implied by a currency board) and second, by preserving degrees of freedom so as to manage a smooth reversal of the initial appreciation in ways that would not disturb stabilization and the deindexation effort. They kept in mind the caveat (Obstfeld, 1995, p. 171) that "it is perilous to rely on the exchange rate as a principal long term instrument for reducing chronic high inflation," but also learned to appreciate the extent to which the foreign-exchange "anchor" heightened the importance of fiscal discipline as the ultimate factor in sustaining stabilization and forced the political establishment to work toward this goal.

While reforms moved along, a gradual devaluation started after May 1995 within a regime fairly deserving of John Williamson's (1999) designation of "crawling bands," and the idea of a one-shot corrective devaluation lost appeal. The international environment seemed friendly from the second half of 1995 on; inflation was falling below 20 percent; and Brazilians seemed unsympathetic to the idea that an apparently smart and rather risky large and discrete devaluation would replace or reduce much of the hard work needed to create economic change. In fact, a devaluation was commonly pledged as an alternative to reform by both its left- and right-wing opponents—namely, the old industrial establishment together with segments of organized labor, both of which were challenged by liberalization and were accustomed to living with high inflation and a weak currency.

Both the Asian crisis in October 1997 and the turbulence started by the Russian moratorium in August 1998 hit Brazil very hard, creating external constraints within which Brazil's stabilization and reform strategies would have to be defined. The Asian crisis was surpassed, however, by a domestic policy mix that failed to materialize as promised and could not produce a viable fiscal package. In view of this breakdown, the turbulence initiated by the Russian moratorium found Brazil very fragile in the eyes of the markets, and there was no alternative to negotiating an agreement with the IMF.

The IMF agreement was meant to be the first of a new kind of arrangement, a "precautionary" program to prevent a major devaluation in Brazil and thus stop contagion of other Latin American countries with good records of market-oriented reforms. The IMF would coordinate the program, which was supported by twenty countries and by up to US$41.5 billion.[4] Much to the surprise of everyone involved in this effort, however, less than a month after the disbursement of the first tranche of the loan, worth US$9.2 billion, and less than a month before the disbursement of a second tranche in the same amount, the governor of the Banco Central do Brasil was replaced and the currency was allowed to float. The exchange rate moved from R$1.22 to a frightening R$2.16, before it stabilized at about R$1.65 to R$1.70. Because the move to a float was by no means planned, some crucial policy definitions are still in the making. The mechanics of the new inflation-targets regime, the fiscal stance, and the exchange-rate regime itself are by no means entirely settled. Perceptions are that a fully flexible exchange-rate regime may deliver too much appreciation if confidence returns as intended, and that it may also produce too much depreciation if, for instance, something happens to Argentina. It would seem that, yet again, new circumstances may require a new balance between exchange-rate flexibility and commitments affecting the real exchange rate. Throughout the 1993–99 period, this balance has had to be constantly revised in response to changing international and domestic conditions. The regime's adaptability to circumstances, rather than the exchange-rate flexibility, is precisely what makes the Brazilian experience an interesting case through which to examine the increasingly popular theory that emerging markets should be on either a currency board or a pure float, with all intermediate alternatives being of questionable viability. In order to reach this point, however, it is necessary to go back in time, to the beginning, and to see how events have evolved since May 1993, when President Fernando Henrique Cardoso was named finance minister and the Real Plan began to be conceived.

This essay is organized as follows. The next section clarifies some generally neglected issues of measurement that emerged in the context

[4] Here and throughout "billion" equals one thousand million.

of the monetary reform initiating the Real Plan and that produced ⨉
some misreading of the initial results of the plan. Sections 3 and 4
discuss relative-price changes inherent to stabilization, the extent of
appreciation associated with the Real Plan, and whether equilibrium
exchange rates should change as the economy moves away from hyperinflation. Section 5 considers the choice of the exchange-rate regime,
keeping in mind the complex agenda of stabilization and reforms to be
met by the Real Plan. Section 6 addresses specific issues raised by the
Asian crisis. Section 7 discusses the policy developments up to the
aftermath of the 1999 devaluation. A conclusion puts events into
perspective and considers the long-term implications of the choices and
events of the years examined.

2 The Measurement of Real Exchange Rates

There are a number of ways to discuss the effects of Brazil's exchange-
rate policy and the specific issues raised by the Real Plan. It is useful
to start with proper measurement. Assessing real-exchange rates under
very high inflation is a complicated matter, especially in the moment of
transition from high to low inflation, and especially when the country
undergoes a currency reform that is considerably richer than simply
cutting the number of zeros. The methodology by which price indices
are constructed is designed to iron out unsystematic price fluctuations
so as to picture the generalized piece of the increase in the price level.
There has been considerable debate recently about the proper measurement of inflation in the presence of changes in technology and
consumer preferences that might create upward biases in price indices
(for example, Shapiro and Wilcox, 1996). There should be no question
that these phenomena are much more severe in Brazil, where the
existing thermometers have been built for very high temperatures and
show little precision under levels of inflation not seen in Brazil since
the 1950s. Relevant as it may be, however, any discussion of measurement in Brazil has had to yield to the overwhelming methodological
problems produced by the sharp change in the price level at the
moment of stabilization, its impact on indexation rules, and associated
repercussions.

Averaging is a useful way to defuse noise and relative-price changes
in the construction of price indices. Inflation is usually computed by
averaging price readings over one period and comparing the results to
the previous average. Simple as it may seem, however, some interesting
problems may occur in periods of transition from high to low inflation

7

or when units of measurement are changed by a currency reform. Figure 1 shows that, in the case of a sudden interruption of inflation, conventional indices might show substantial inflation, even though the price level remains constant from day one of the program.

The line in Figure 1 shows the price level, which ceases to grow as we enter July. Yet, July inflation is computed by the comparison of the average price level in July (point B) with the average price level in June (point A).[5] Thus measured, inflation is positive, despite the price level's being constant during July by virtue of what may be called a statistical-carryover effect that has no economic meaning whatsoever. It does seem as though "July inflation" is a misnomer, but this is the way inflation is measured in real life. In the concrete situation of July 1994 Brazil, if this residual inflation, or statistical carryover, had not been extracted from the official measures for inflation, it would have severely distorted expectations and all nominal values subject to formal or informal indexation clauses.

The magnitude of these distortions—seen in Table 1—may be such that their impact on expectations, relative prices, and legal claims under indexed contracts will cancel an otherwise successful stabilization, because there may be "massive and unintended wealth redistribution between debtors and creditors, with ensuing risks of numerous failures and financial instability" (Dornbusch and Simonsen, 1987, pp. 15–16). The apparently simple solution of resorting to point-to-point indices—that is, instant comparisons of the price level at specific points

FIGURE 1

INFLATION AFTER STABILIZATION

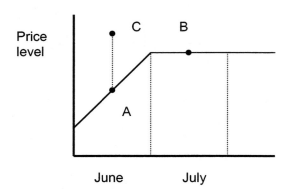

[5] In Brazil, there are usually three or four rounds of price collection within a month, resulting in weekly releases of monthly (four-week) inflation rates.

8

TABLE 1

GETÚLIO VARGAS FOUNDATION INDICES OF ALTERNATIVE INFLATION RATES,
JULY AND AUGUST, 1994
(*Percent*)

	IGP-DI		IPA-DI		IPC-BR		INCC	
	Dirty	Clean	Dirty	Clean	Dirty	Clean	Dirty	Clean
July	24.70	5.47	23.10	4.41	32.40	8.10	10.30	3.58
August	3.34	3.34	4.40	4.40	2.60	2.60	0.14	0.14
	IGP-M		IPA-M		IPC-M		INCC-M	
	Dirty	Clean	Dirty	Clean	Dirty	Clean	Dirty	Clean
July	40.00	4.33	36.90	2.40	44.50	7.61	42.80	4.89
August	7.56	3.94	7.87	3.98	8.16	4.56	3.95	1.72

NOTE: IGPs are weighted averages of IPAs (wholesale prices), IPCs (consumer prices), and INCCs (construction materials) having weights of 0.6, 0.3 and 0.1, respectively. IGP-DI refers to prices collected between the first and thirtieth of each month, and IGP-M refers to prices collected between the twenty-first of the previous month and the twentieth of the month of reference and available on the last day of the month.
SOURCES: Depec-Banco Central do Brasil; Fundação Getúlio Vargas.

of time without any averaging—produces results that are very risky and in many cases impossible to implement in practice.[6] In order to prevent these distortions, mechanisms of deindexation, *tablitas* and currency reforms, are usually designed to secure relative-price neutrality during the transition.[7]

This classic problem in high-inflation stabilization appeared in the Real Plan in a slightly different form, which may be explained as follows. Suppose that, in the situation described by Figure 1, the exchange rate was modified daily according to the best estimates of *current* inflation,[8] and that, entering July, the dollar was adopted as

[6] Prices included in indices are not continuously read every day. Sampling processes and interpolations are commonly used, rendering a continuous series for the price level difficult to construct. In addition, the publication of point-to-point indices (done by the Fundação Instituto de Pesquisas Econômicas [FIPE] for the consumer-price index [IPC] for the city of São Paulo) revealed alarming degrees of volatility. This volatility explains the very strong resistance to the use of such indices in indexation provisions.

[7] The paper by Dornbusch and Simonsen (1987) is one among many explaining the problem of, and providing the rationale for, deindexation measures.

[8] This means that the central bank was working with the best estimate of "current" inflation, or with the rates to be released two to three weeks ahead.

the national currency, the old currency being replaced by the new on the first day of July at the market rate (say, $2,750 units of the old currency for each unit of the new currency). The price level within July would then be directly measured in dollars, the new national currency, and, the July inflation would thus have to be measured in the new currency.[9] But how could the price level in dollars in July be compared to the price-level readings of the previous month? Figure 1 does not help in this case, because there is a currency discontinuity as we enter July, for which the units of measurement are different from those available to measure the price level in June. To reinstate comparability, we would have to take all past price readings and convert them into dollars. But at what rate? Should they all be converted at the exchange rate of the day of transition ($2,750)? Or should they be converted into dollars using the exchange rates on the day to which they refer?

The answers to these questions direct us back to the issue of eliminating the statistical carryover: if we were to choose to convert all past price readings (from June) by the exchange rate of the D-day, $2,750, it would be exactly like comparing B with A. If, instead, we were to recover the past dollar prices, by converting readings in the old currency by the exchange rate *on the day prices were collected*, the comparison would be between B and C, this being the inflation rate in the new currency, or the dollar inflation rate, or the loss of the new currency's purchasing power in terms of goods in the month of July. Thus, the July inflation rate in the new currency (in dollars in the example) would capture the acceleration of inflation in the old currency, or the excess inflation that was not captured by the exchange-rate depreciation. Note that, even though the mechanism used in Brazil was very similar, Brazil did not adopt the dollar as the national currency. Four months before the issuance of the new currency, a unit of account called "unidade real de valor" (URV) was created and considerable effort was expended to make it the sole index for all indexation provisions. Because the URV was readjusted daily according to current inflation, just as the exchange rate was, it maintained a constant exchange rate with respect to the dollar. On July 1, 1994, the URV was issued as a full currency, and its name was changed to "real." At this point, the real was allowed to float

[9] Recall that the legal framework for indexation is based on the assumption that a given nominal claim has its value reduced by the loss of purchasing power of the currency and so needs to be rebuilt in order to avoid undue wealth debasement.

with respect to the dollar. This, in brief, is how the Brazilian currency reform was built.[10]

The choices regarding the measurement of inflation are obviously crucial for the formation of expectations during the first few weeks of the new currency and for the proper execution of all indexation provisions. They are also critical for all computations of real exchange rates and associated judgments on currency valuation and sustainability of the new plan. The legal instruments establishing the new currency stated very clearly that, for indexation purposes, only inflation rates computed without statistical residuals could be valid.[11] Pursuant to this, all research institutes responsible for the manufacturing of price indices in Brazil reported their inflation rates for the months of July and August 1994. Some of them, for the sake of transparency, or in response to the interests of those funding the indices, also released "dirty" indices contaminated by the statistical carryover.[12]

Table 1 shows the difference between "clean" and "dirty" inflation rates for some of the most commonly used FGV indices. For the most popular indices—weighted averages of wholesale, consumer, and construction prices collected between the first and thirtieth days of the month (IGP-DI) and weighted averages of wholesale, consumer, and construction prices collected between the twenty-first day of the previous month and the twentieth day of the month of reference (IGP-M)— the residual inflation, that is, the difference between clean and dirty indices for July and August combined, is 18.2 percent and 38.9 percent, respectively. These magnitudes highlight the importance of the legal dispositions precluding the use of dirty indices in indexation provisions. One wonders, however, whether the transparency gained by releasing these dirty figures outweighs the problems created by their misuse. Researchers unfamiliar with the problems could very well use

---

[10] The similarities between the mechanism just described and that underlying the German Rentenmark experience in November 1923 should not be missed.

[11] A fascinating discussion on the legal issues involved in setting the rules for the conversion of obligations into a new currency is provided by Frederick Mann (1992, parts I and II).

[12] The Getúlio Vargas Foundation (FGV), a traditional provider of price indices, was one such institution. The indices released by the FGV should be used very carefully, especially for comparisons of readings before and after the Real Plan, because their cumulative price levels include statistical residuals for July and August 1994. A curious way out of the distortion is to use an exchange-rate series that is also constructed with residuals.

the dirty indices to form judgments about the performance of inflation and, on that basis, to compute real exchange rates and assess their sustainability.[13]

There were several instances of preliminary assessments of the Real Plan based on dirty versions of price indices, some resulting in dramatic statements. Over time, as these methodological details came to be better understood, judgments changed. One wonders, however, how many audiences were terrified by the "around 40 percent overvalued" warnings issued loudly on screens worldwide until perceptions about the real's feasibility were revised. This is not to say that there should be no diversity of views on the Real Plan, for the most varied reasons, but proper methods of measurement could have avoided much unnecessary noise about Brazilian exchange-rate policies.

3   Relative Prices and Equilibrium Exchange Rates

As during all high-inflation stabilization episodes, striking differences occurred during the Real Plan between inflation rates measured by the available consumer-price indices (CPIs) and those measured by the producer-price indices (wholesale-price indices [WPIs]). Evidence that this was so has been extensively discussed and duly recognized (Franco, 1995, chaps. 12 and 13; Dornbusch, 1997, p. 381; Fishlow, 1997, table 2.2). These relative-price changes are relevant to gauging the success of the Real Plan, for the same reasons that proper measurements are: the plan's success ultimately hinges on what the rate of inflation was. Yet, defining the relevant rate of inflation requires a far-from-inconsequential choice among indices displaying sharply contrasting behaviors. Judgments about the sustainability of Brazilian policies depend crucially on this choice. According to Fishlow (1997, p. 54), for instance, were we to use WPIs instead of CPIs, we would "bring the Real Plan within the margin of probable success rather than undoubted failure." We know that different indices measure different things and serve different purposes. There should be a criterion for choosing either WPIs or CPIs as the preferred index to assess the success of stabilization. Similarly, there should be a reason for the choice of indices to be used in the computation of real exchange rates. The question is, are we better

---

[13] As we consider longer periods from the past, we should recall that Brazil had five currency changes in the ten years prior to the Real Plan, each change producing the very same statistical problems just mentioned. Researchers should be careful in using real-exchange-rate series for longer periods.

served with WPIs or with CPIs? Should there be specific price indices designed for real-exchange-rate computation?

At least as far as normal times are considered, the choice as to whether WPIs or CPIs should be used, and how they should be corrected in measuring competitiveness, is neither new nor conclusive (Edwards, 1989, pp. 5–6).[14] It may be even less conclusive during stabilization, when wide swings in relative prices are occurring, for reasons that are not entirely understood. Indeed, the unusual behavior of CPIs (relative to WPIs) during stabilization episodes, of which the Real Plan is no exception, has puzzled most observers and dissuaded them from working with CPIs. Something would appear to be happening with services (Table 2 below) that produces increases in CPIs that reflect, not inflation, but, rather, a large change in relative prices associated with the stabilization effort. As the economy abandons hyperinflation and adjusts itself to a "normal" life, the huge distortions in resource allocation produced by hyperinflation will not disappear without affecting the price system.[15] How should we consider the relative-price changes occurring under hyperinflation stabilization?

Table 2 shows a substantial increase, for every episode, in the relative price of services and products designated as "differentiable" within the CPIs. This seems to explain, seasonal factors apart, the substantial increase of CPIs relative to WPIs. It is true that WPIs are made of baskets rich in tradables, a fact that makes the measurement of real exchange rates somewhat tautological: in the limit, given perfect competition and the law of one price, there cannot be any change in the real exchange rate thus measured. If there are shortcomings in using CPIs for real-exchange-rate computations during stabilization, the same is true for WPIs, although in the other direction! In any event, the relative increase in CPIs over WPIs is visible in every case shown in the table and certainly extends well beyond the episodes described. It can be argued that this is simply the consequence of appreciation and that all supply-side influences are illusory. It seems reasonable,

---

[14] Dornbusch, Goldfajn, and Valdes (1995, p. 258) argue that on a more general basis, CPIs are "poor guides to competitiveness," because they may be affected by changes, such as the Balassa-Samuelson effect (caused by different rates of growth in productivity in tradables and nontradables) and yield little meaning about what real exchange rates should measure.

[15] One common example of a relative-price correction appearing in almost all episodes is the case of rents. Mechanisms of rent control or legal impediments to the indexation of rents has resulted in significant distortions in this market, distortions that are generally corrected after stabilization through deregulation or recontracting.

TABLE 2

Inflation in the First Four Months Following Several Stabilization Plans
(Cumulative percentage change)

Items[a]	IPC-r Shares Aug 1994	Cruzado Mar-Jun 1986	Bresser Jul-Oct 1987	Verão Feb-May 1989	Collor Apr-Jul 1990	Collor-2 Mar-Jun 1991	Cavallo Apr-Jul 1991	Real Jul-Oct 1994
IPC (CPIs)	—	3.37	26.46	29.67	54.71	38.80	14.76	15.67
Food	31.37	-2.36	19.43	15.08	32.44	25.15	21.18	15.61
Industrials	10.28	-2.20	18.95	16.69	28.97	10.72	4.79	3.49
Public prices	12.36	-2.64	22.27	12.65	42.07	22.67	7.67	10.82
Seasonal	3.42	-5.06	24.21	80.73	110.78	53.52	26.66	56.32
Services	9.96	12.61	50.03	49.93	139.60	91.51	21.71	37.82
Differentiable	21.04	14.12	28.02	51.83	78.55	43.87	13.92	19.37
IPA (WPIs)	100.00	-1.73	35.98	33.27	44.27	34.45	4.63	9.34[b]
Agriculture	30.36	1.27	57.82	72.03	136.72	62.81	32.91	28.94[b]
Industrials	69.64	-2.80	30.52	20.87	24.80	23.45	1.59	0.99[b]

NOTE: IPC-r is a special version of the INPC-IBGE. Cruzado, Bresser, Verão, Collor, and Collor-2 refer to stabilization plans implemented in Brazil. Cavallo refers to the Argentina Convertibility Plan.

[a] The Food group includes rice, pasta, sugar, meat, eggs, milk, coffee, bread, soy derivatives, and other foodstuffs; Industrials includes cleaning and hygiene products, refreshments, beer, cigarettes, pharmaceuticals, and new cars; Public prices includes land taxes, water, sewage, public services, gasoline, public transportation, and education; Seasonal includes vegetables, roots, fruits, and fish; Services includes rent, condominium, auto repair, personal services, and clubs; and Differentiable includes used cars, clothing, shoes, textiles, restaurants, fast food, and electronics. The composition of different indices is adapted for comparability.

[b] August to November.

SOURCES: Depec- and Indec-Banco Central do Brasil; Getúlio Vargas Foundation (FGV); Instituto Brasileiro de Geografia e Estatística (IBGE); and Cunha (1990).

however, to consider that something happens with regard to search-intensive goods, for instance, because the dispersion of relative prices falls dramatically, or that something happens with regard to real wages following the alleviation of the distributive tensions after stabilization. What, after all, is the best way to measure real exchange rates?

Figure 2 presents three alternative measures for the real exchange rate from January 1988 through December 1999. The most commonly used index in Brazil is the one regularly published by Fundação Centro de Estudos de Comércio Exterior (Funcex), a privately funded think tank that has traditionally supplied foreign-trade statistics. The Funcex index is calculated using WPIs (for the United States, PPIs), to measure world inflation, and using the FGV WPIs to account for Brazilian inflation. The figure shows a second index computed with CPIs for

14

FIGURE 2

THREE MEASURES OF REAL EXCHANGE RATES, 1988–1999

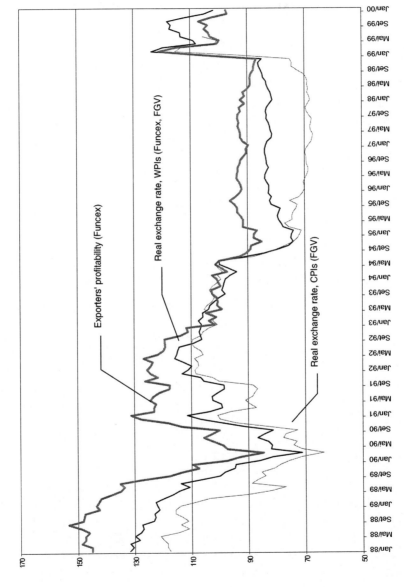

both domestic and international inflation, and it shows a third index as well, known as "exporters' profitability" (EP), also published by Funcex on a regular basis. Exporters' profitability is actually a real-exchange-rate index for which exporters' prices replace international inflation and exporters' costs replace domestic inflation. Indices for prices and costs (including wages) are measured directly for the twenty-eight predominant export sectors for which disaggregated data are available and use weights given by the 1992 Input Output Table. Exporters' profitability is possibly the most carefully made direct measure of competitiveness released on a regular basis (for methodological detail, see Guimarães, Pourchet, and Markwald, 1997).

The behavior of these three indices differs in several ways. As expected, because CPI inflation was larger than WPI inflation in the first few years of the Real Plan, real exchange rates using CPIs show a much greater appreciation. It may also be seen that the relation between CPIs and WPIs started to revert slowly through time in Brazil, as it did in countries such as Argentina and Mexico, although not to the extent necessary to undo the change experienced during the early years of stabilization.

Of the three indices, the EP index shows the lowest appreciation at the moment of stabilization, a finding that may suggest that the nominal-exchange-rate appreciation was partly offset by increases in exporters' prices or by reductions in their costs. Certainly, the comparison of EP with the other indices provokes an interesting discussion of the pass-through process. The extent to which Brazilian exporters could actually shift the impact of nominal appreciation by changing their prices appears to be significant in light of the 11.6 percent increase in the aggregate price index of Brazilian exports between June and October 1994, when prices of basic products increased by 17.1 percent and prices of semimanufactured and manufactured products increased by 13.2 percent and 8.9 percent. For the twelve months following June 1994, aggregate export prices increased by 17.9 percent, and prices for basic, semimanufactured, and manufactured products increased by 9.7 percent, 30.9 percent, and 19.3 percent, respectively. Export-price behavior after the 1999 devaluation would seem to confirm the same pattern of an inverse correlation between changes in exchange rates and terms of trade. During 1999, aggregate export prices decreased by 12.2 percent, and prices for basic, semimanufactured, and manufactured products decreased by 15.4 percent, 13.9 percent, and 10.9 percent, respectively.

16

Swings this large in the terms of trade are not common in Brazil. International evidence from empirical studies of the pass-through process seems to support the notion that an incomplete pass-through, of about 60 percent on average, is the most likely explanation (compare Goldberg and Knetter, 1997, p. 1250). This incompleteness may even have been enhanced if—as is plausible to assume in the Brazilian case—perceptions were that exchange-rate swings were temporary or if there were significant segmentation and market power in Brazilian exports. Rigorously speaking, however, the matter of whether this was a favorable coincidence (or an exogenous change in the terms of trade) in both 1994 and 1999, or whether it was an incomplete pass-through to offset the nominal appreciation or depreciation is a matter that can only be resolved by a more specific empirical analysis.

It is interesting to observe also that, over time, EP recovered more quickly than the other measures of real exchange rates. Although there is no reason to presume that the gradual devaluation policy implemented after March 1995 would affect any of the indices differently, it is true that EP may be reflecting productivity increases not necessarily captured in the other indices. Productivity growth was very high, indeed, during these years of trade liberalization—an average of 7.5 percent a year from 1990 to 1998 for labor productivity and 3.4 percent a year from 1991 to 1997 for total factor productivity (see Table 7, on p. 85, for more detail). Productivity increases are important in discussing a number of issues pertaining to growth and distribution, but exactly how should productivity growth interfere with real-exchange-rate measurement?

It can be argued that the presence of rapid productivity growth for a prolonged period of time eventually dismisses the discussion about exchange-rate (over)valuation, because real exchange rates *corrected* by productivity differentials will have been devaluing spontaneously and significantly through time. This may explain why, for instance, the issue of exchange-rate overvaluation in Argentina is so often ignored, even by champions of devaluation. On the other extreme, observers such as Dornbusch (1997, p. 385) suggest that productivity growth is a gimmick on which "official allegations" are based in order to evade the crucial issue, which is that "when trying to explain why a particular real exchange rate is not overvalued, governments often point to productivity gains." Dornbusch's claim may be based on the idea that all productivity gains are reflected in computations of purchasing-power parity, because gains are entirely passed into prices (Dornbusch, Goldfajn, and Valdes, 1995, p. 258). This may well be false, however, because productivity gains may be passed into wages or profit margins, which would result in

17

differences between competitiveness measures that are based on prices, such as real exchange rates, and direct measures, such as EP (see Figure 2).

A substantial portion of productivity gains were passed on to wages in the early years of stabilization (see Figure 3). This phenomenon was helped somewhat by difficulties in avoiding some residual indexation to wages, but it was also contained by the nature of adjustments implied in the typical program followed by the average firm—a program comprised mostly of reorganization of the workspace, improved quality control, and managerial innovations, with little additional investment in fixed capital and with significant reductions in employment (see Salm, Saboia, and de Carvalho, 1997). This significant increase in real wages should not be seen as *wasted* productivity gains or as an indication of populist inclinations in the Real Plan;[16] the increases in productivity relieved already existing distributive tensions with little inflationary effect. Indeed, the sharp increase in wages seen after the Real Plan can be viewed as a natural consequence of the acute distributive tensions that developed as Brazil moved toward democracy in the late 1980s and that could not be resolved in view of budget imbalances and inflation. It is only an apparent paradox, however, that neoliberal reforms, particularly trade liberalization and stabilization, could create the conditions for a much better income distribution, a cause normally supported above any other by the anti-neoliberal left. It appears that profit margins have increased their share of the productive gains over time (Figure 3 shows that the slope of the productivity line is steep compared with the evolution of wages). This increase should help the cause of Brazilian exports by affecting, for instance, the dynamics of firms' entry into, and exit from, exporting activity.

One should note that all three measures in Figure 2 show significant, if different, degrees of appreciation at the onset of the plan. All three also show some recovery over time, by virtue of the policy of gradual devaluation, and, in the case of EP, by virtue also of the impact of productivity change. In January 1999, when the devaluation was initiated, the appreciation was—using the figure for June 1994 as a benchmark—24.9 percent, if measured by CPIs, and 13.1 percent and 15 percent, if measured by EPs and WPIs, respectively. Comparing the average of the first semester before the Real Plan with the last quarter before the

---

[16] It should also be mentioned that to the very extent that inflation can be seen as a tax on money holders, it can be argued that the elimination of hyperinflation represents a tax rebate (given mostly to low-income wage earners) that results in a wage increase.

FIGURE 3

WAGES IN DOLLARS AND THE LABOR-PRODUCTIVITY INDEX

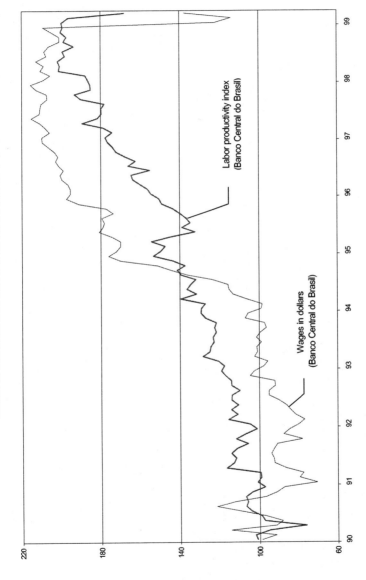

devaluation (October to December 1998), the picture changes little: appreciation measured by CPIs was at 25.4 percent, and appreciation measured by EP and WPIs was at 12.9 percent and 12.1 percent, respectively.

The 1999 devaluation had different impacts on the three indices. The initial overshooting was weaker for the EP index and the ensuing appreciation was stronger, because it captured the loss in export prices mentioned above. Because the WPI inflation was much higher in 1999 (about 30 percent) than the CPI inflation (all indices at one-digit levels), the real devaluation appears much larger in the CPI-based measure of real exchange rates than in the WPI-based measure. Taking the averages for the first semester of 1994 as benchmarks, the real devaluations shown by the EP, CPI-deflated, and WPI-deflated indices in January 2000 were –2.7 percent, ... percent, and 4.5 percent, respectively. Using December 1999 as the benchmark, the real devaluations shown in January 2000 were 10.6 percent, ... percent, and 19.8 percent, respectively—not far, after all the swings during 1999, from the levels where it would have been had the old crawl been maintained.

4 Appreciation and the End of High Inflation

Appreciation seems ubiquitous in stabilization episodes. In the specific case of the Real Plan, the question to ask is whether appreciation relative to some past benchmark—let it be June 1994, the twelve months prior to July 1994, or the average for 1992—necessarily means overvaluation. In view of the omnipresence of appreciation at the end of high-inflation episodes, the question is simple: is appreciation an intrinsic feature of the stabilization process? Should we expect the currency to grow stronger as the country overcomes hyperinflation? Is appreciation in some sense an equilibrium outcome?

Traditional explanations for the phenomenon, generally addressing the experience of the Southern Cone countries in the 1970s, have assumed that appreciation is an unintended and inconvenient consequence of a stabilization—and of prefixed devaluation schedules, to be precise—conducted under backward-looking price-setting behavior or under less-than-perfect credibility for the new policies (see Roldós, 1995, and Rebelo and Végh, 1995). More recently, and mostly in view of the experience of the successor states of the former Soviet Union, it is argued that "the supply side effects of disinflation proved to be an essential component of any scenario that comes to mimicking actual stabilization dynamics" (Rebelo and Végh, 1995, p. 127). It is significant

20

that the supply-side designation is being used very broadly, possibly to refer to factors that are not strictly monetary but that are recognized as relevant in view of the gigantic real or structural changes taking place. This is naturally accepted in the cases of transition economies, but it is not difficult to claim the same treatment for instances of Latin American hyperinflation and for Brazil in particular. In fact, it would be hard to admit that a dislocation as large as a hyperinflation will be absolutely neutral with respect to real variables, or to be more specific, that the same equilibrium values for real wages, exchange rates, and interest rates will prevail as the economy moves from an inflation rate of 45 percent a month to a rate of 3 percent a year. With all due respect to the neutrality of money, it would take a maverick monetarist interpretation of the Brazilian inflation, and of any hyperinflation episode, to presume that something will not happen with real variables in a transition of this magnitude.

Yet, policymakers know remarkably little about supply-side effects during big disinflations and about changes in relative prices (of nontradable goods) in particular. There are different forces at work, structural (or supply-side) as well as macroeconomic, and the recent efforts to account for their relative importance, such as the study by Rebelo and Végh (1995), even though right about the direction of things, do not come close to the orders of magnitude the phenomenon acquires in real episodes: "large consumption booms and the sizeable real appreciations are puzzling" (Rebelo and Végh, 1995, p. 168). In addition, the pattern of relative-price change shown in Table 2 would appear to suggest that there is something more about services than simply their nontradable character.[17] But what are the specific economic mechanisms at work and how should policymakers react? Should this be seen as a currency overvaluation to be avoided or corrected or as a relative-price accommodation with which to comply? Is this a monetary or a real (supply-side) phenomenon? Could a stronger currency be a natural outcome of a successful stabilization?

There are surely many ways to discuss the Real Plan, and the procedure adopted here does not claim generality (for a more detailed presentation, see Franco, 1995, chap. 4). In order to describe the

---

[17] One possibility is related to the different pricing dynamics for services and goods. With stabilization, there would be a significant reduction in the expected rewards from search behavior, which are proportional to relative-price dispersion. Because services are more search intensive, they would tend to become more expensive as consumers would be increasingly tied to customer relationships and less willing to search.

policy options chosen in the real-life situation in Brazil, the following discussion targets specific mechanisms and institutional features of the Brazilian economy, such as dollarization (widespread indexation) and acute distributive tensions, that may not be found elsewhere. Figure 4 shows two relationships: the first, BP, expresses external balance, or different combinations of the current and capital account, for which a crucial element is a phenomenon known as currency substitution or dollarization. It refers to the fact, very common in high-inflation countries, that, independent of (real-) interest-rate differentials, residents shelter a large share (larger as inflation rises) of their wealth in dollars or dollar-denominated assets, in order to bypass local inflation. As inflation advances, the real exchange rate has to depreciate in order for an additional current-account surplus to develop and finance, or "transfer," the capital flight.[18]

The second relationship, PP, describes the wage-price-devaluation spiral in high-inflation conditions. It shows that inflation accelerates if wages are less than the amount targeted by unions, or that a high *level* of inflation is needed to frustrate workers' desires, because wages are always the slowest moving link in the devaluation-inflation spiral. This relationship involves the notion of a "distributive conflict" or recalls the notion of a "100 percent plus indexation" (Modigliani and Padoa-Schioppa, 1978), which may seem a little old-fashioned to mainstream

FIGURE 4

EQUILIBRIUM INFLATION AND THE REAL EXCHANGE RATE

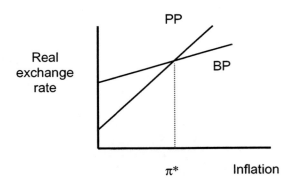

[18] A similar relationship, although developed in a somewhat more sophisticated framework, is provided by Calvo, Reinhart, and Végh (1994). Their argument is that, under less-than-ideal fiscal conditions, governments targeting the real exchange rate would have to accept rates of inflation higher than they otherwise would, or that, under high inflation, the exchange rate would tend to be undervalued.

macroeconomists, but there should be no question that it is one of the distinctive features of extreme inflation (see Dornbusch, Sturzenegger, and Wolf, 1990).

The high-inflation equilibrium pictured in Figure 4 has two important characteristics: (1) the exchange rate is very low (undervalued?), so that a large current-account surplus finances a large deficit in the capital account, as is typically seen in hyperinflation, and (2) the real wage is lower than targeted values, thus producing a chronic pressure on nominal wages and keeping the well-known wage-price-depreciation spiral on the move.[19] Note that, given the slopes of the two relationships, there is a macroeconomic *inconsistency* at zero inflation: the real exchange rate (wages) consistent with external balance is too high (low) compared with the levels desired by workers.[20] If, in this model, inflation is *artificially* brought down, say, by a price or exchange-rate freeze, the economy will, all other policies prevailing, move momentarily to point B (Figure 5). In the absence of any other shift in policies, however, the macroeconomic inconsistency will reproduce again the high-inflation equilibrium at point A. This is an important aspect of the 1980s Brazilian stabilization experience, which included several episodes of heterodoxy, aptly described by the late Mario Henrique Simonsen as "anesthesia without surgery." In the absence of changes in macroeconomic fundamentals, inflation has always returned with a vengeance.

The model is helpful in explaining the chain of events during the Real Plan (see Franco, 1995, chap. 1 for a precise record of the events). The program starts with a complex deindexation mechanism

[19] There seems to be little question among observers of Brazilian inflation that distributive tensions play a major role in the process. This should not be surprising, given the levels of inequality exhibited by Brazil. Several models have been developed to exploit different aspects of this problem. Among these are distributive-conflict models that are easy to reconcile with orthodox models so long as one accepts that "a large fiscal deficit . . . often reflects a country's inability to resolve social conflicts over income and wealth distribution" (Bruno, 1993, p. 252). For a survey of these "consensus" models for Brazil, see Bacha (1988).

[20] The usual objection to distributive-conflict models for hyperinflations, or for inflation more generally, is that rational agents learn how the process works, so that something will happen in the labor market in order to block it. In practice, however, institutional constraints seem to be paramount: the frustration of unions is a solid feature of every episode of high inflation. On a more general level, one can always argue that processes of inflation are not rational, that they are the outcome of a collective decision process that need not display individual rationality. Attempts to look at social-crisis episodes and hyperinflations as outcomes of the rational behavior of an omniscient and malign government seeking to maximize revenues from money creation belong in the realm of fantasy.

23

FIGURE 5

THE MECHANICS OF STABILIZATION

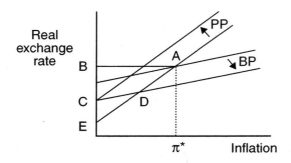

centered on the URV and meant to stop inflation and to preserve distributive (relative-price) neutrality during at least the first moments of the transition. Although a simplification, the model helps us to imagine that we are fixing the exchange rate into an economy in which all prices and wages are, on a daily basis, subject to exchange-rate indexation; that is, we work within the framework of a *dollarized* economy.[21] It also helps to consider that the only difference between the Real Plan and the previous cases of heterodoxy are that the fundamentals were duly addressed in the Real Plan; that is, the enabling monetary and fiscal policies allowed both the BP and PP curves of Figure 4 to shift so as to support an equilibrium at C with zero inflation (Figure 5). Yet, because the price level does not change as quickly as the exchange rate, the economy actually moves rapidly to point B, where the real exchange rate is so low (depreciated) or the trade (current-account) surplus is so high that, in the absence of capital flights previously triggered by high inflation, there is a sizable external surplus, a strong pressure toward appreciation, and a significant reserve accumulation. The economy should find its way toward the new equilibrium at C, where the exchange rate has appreciated considerably in

[21] Because the Real Plan tried to reproduce this mechanism of fixing the exchange rate under dollarization, it is often described as an "exchange-rate-based stabilization." This description should be taken with a grain of salt, however. Brazil was by no means a dollarized economy, either in terms of offshore wealth as a percentage of domestic financial wealth or in terms of indexation practiced with respect to the dollar. The artificial dollarization created by the introduction of the URV was only a coordination device, not actual dollarization (see Franco, 1995, chap. 1, for details).

real terms, wages are higher, and the trade balance is lower with respect to the original equilibrium at A. At C, there is external balance at the level of the real wages (exchange rates) targeted by the unions.

This successful landing at point C describes the first phase of the Real Plan, which was completed during the third quarter of 1994. The sustainability issue then immediately arises, because at C, interest rates are kept high, but other expansionary influences seem to overheat the economy. These are (1) the inflation-tax rebate—that is, the impact of the redistributive effect of stabilization on absorption, (2) the emergence from poverty of 15 million new consumers, resulting in new opportunities for indebtedness and a boom in consumer credit much welcomed by banks in need of new business frontiers, and (3) some relaxation of fiscal policy induced by the inadequacy of public budgets for a stable price environment.[22] These influences, if strong enough, could put both curves back to point A and result in the real's failure. Indeed, the crucial challenge of any stabilization is in dealing with its own initial success, especially when the economy is booming, the future looks bright, and political willingness to entertain sacrifices is at its lowest point.

The recommended policy response to these circumstances would be a tightening that, if purely fiscal, would mostly shift PP further up, and, if purely monetary, would mostly shift BP further down.[23] If we think of an equilibrium at C and expansionary influences as shifting PP downward, the no-response alternative would give us equilibrium at D. A fiscal-policy response would bring us back to C, and a monetary-policy response would put the economy at E, in a classic crowding-out situation. At E, the exchange rate appreciates further and creates (or aggravates) the twin-deficits problem, that is, large budget and current-account deficits prevail as mirror images of one another. With budget deficits unchanged, interest rates cannot fall, the economy becomes depressed, and the perception of fragility is established. A similar situation occurs in response to an external shock, that is, an upward shift in the BP curve, whereby a fiscal response shifts PP upward, and

[22] The relation between fiscal policy and inflation in Brazil is complex. Indexation has been very effective with respect to tax collection but rather ineffective with respect to spending (that is, with respect to budget allocations). The transition to stable prices causes an increase in the budget deficit (Bacha, 1994; Franco, 1995, chaps. 8–10).

[23] For simplicity, we may proceed as though monetary policy affects only the BP curve. This may not be entirely correct, given its effects on absorption, but we lose very little by ignoring that.

equilibrium obtains at zero inflation and at a higher (more depreciated) exchange rate. If the response is purely monetary (raising interest rates), BP should be shifted all the way back to where it was, at the same real exchange rate but with a more precarious external position being sustained by high interest rates that cannot fall.

The model highlights the importance of fiscal policy for determining what the final equilibrium will be, how sustainable it will be, and what will happen to interest rates and the activity level. The Brazilian authorities assumed that actions affecting fiscal policy would be gradual, given their "reform" nature, and would be implemented simultaneously with interest-rate reductions, thus slowly negating the crowding-out impact. In parallel, trade reform would be producing significant rates of growth in productivity, which would enhance competitiveness and would also relieve the distributive conflict. Productivity gains would push PP downward, creating a deflationary bias and some room for a devaluation of more or less the same magnitude, with no inflationary impact, thus further helping external balance.

If monetary policy were to carry the burden of stabilization, however, with fiscal adjustment mostly absent, low inflation would probably prevail, at the cost of a chronically tight monetary policy and a depressed economy. This might rightly be seen as a fragile stabilization, or a situation in which the exchange rate would be hard to defend. Even if the exchange-rate anchor were removed, the fiscal deficit would prevent much of the decrease in interest rates, and the economy might be subject to considerable volatility. If, instead, fiscal policy were the basis of the stabilization effort, the economy would be more likely to reach a stronger or more sustainable equilibrium, for it would stabilize at lower interest rates. Either way, there would be an appreciation at the onset of the stabilization program.

Because the chief goal was to make this new equilibrium sustainable, the appreciation of the exchange rate with respect to its position immediately before the stabilization should not necessarily have meant, at least in the beginning, that the currency had become overvalued or that the rate was incorrect. In fact, any stabilization program, and not just those specifically based on exchange rates, can be accused of relying "on currency overvaluation to artificially reduce inflation" (Edwards, 1997, p. 102), especially if the program fails. (If it works, well, that is because the fundamentals were properly addressed!) At a distance, one fails to distinguish artificial appreciations from those warranted by new fundamentals. In fact, one could go so far as to say that all initial appreciations are artificial, because the required reforms

26

are always in the future. The successful programs are the ones capable of addressing fundamentals and turning an artificial into a sustainable exchange rate. It is not always easy to perceive whether or not, and exactly how, fundamental imbalances at the root of hyperinflation are being corrected. These are relevant considerations that go a step beyond assessments made solely on the basis of simple comparisons between the real exchange rate at any point in time, however measured, and the exchange-rate prevailing immediately before the Real Plan or any other arbitrarily chosen baseline.

5 The Exchange-Rate Regime: Choices under Differing Circumstances

What is new with regard to equilibrium exchange rates during a stabilization effort? The issue of sustainability of a given balance-of-payments position has long been discussed with regard to economies variously described as "latecomers," "developing," "tigers" or, lately, "emerging." In fact, these economies earn these designations largely by sustaining investment rates at levels that are consistently higher than the rates supported by domestic savings. There seems to be no question that international borrowing (and lending) raises investment possibilities and that countries trying to accelerate the pace of capital accumulation should consider intensive use of investment, which is one of the advantages brought by globalization. The question is how much is safe or how much is perceived by donors to be safe under varying circumstances. Financial history is replete with episodes of less-than-ideal allegiance to intertemporal budget constraints by borrowers and of reckless risk analysis by lenders. It also provides several examples in which unforeseen events have caused otherwise sound judgments to result in risky, or even disastrous, situations. This issue is relevant for Brazil now and has been for as long as one can remember. Questions have been raised since the beginning of the Real Plan about whether Brazil's current-account deficit is too high, thus exposing the economy unnecessarily to the vagaries of international finance, or whether the plan has restrained economic growth. The old issue appears now in a slightly different form, connected to the dynamics of stabilization and not so closely related to the budget deficits, which are seen as the key issue with respect to Brazil's stabilization and resumption of growth.

Some background for these issues is offered in Table 3. The small current-account surplus shown between 1991 and 1993 had actually developed in the mid–1980s as a forced response to the 1982 debt

TABLE 3

BALANCE-OF-PAYMENTS ITEMS, 1991–1999

(*US$ billions and percent*)

	1991–1993[a]	1994	1995	1996	1997	1st Sem 1998	2nd Sem 1998	1998	Jan-March 1999
Current account	1.4	-1.7	-18.0	-23.1	-33.4	-14.0	-21.0	-35.0	-5.2
As % of GDP	0.3	-0.3	-2.6	-3.0	-4.2	-1.8	-2.7	-4.5	-3.8
Foreign direct investment	1.4	2.6	5.5	10.5	18.7	8.6	17.5	26.1	7.7
As % of global FDI	0.8	1.1	1.7	3.0	4.7	n.a.	n.a.	n.a.	n.a.
Portfolio investment (net)	3.0	7.3	2.3	6.0	5.3	8.3	-10.1	-1.8	0.2
Inflows	15.9	55.3[b]	18.2	27.4	49.1	36.5	23.3	59.8	7.1
Amortization	-8.8	-50.4[b]	-11.0	-14.4	-28.8	-10.6	-23.0	-33.6	-18.2
Other long-term capital (net)	7.1	4.9	7.2	12.9	20.4	25.9	0.3	26.2	-11.1
Other short-term capital (net)	-5.2	-5.8	15.9	2.3	-18.9	-10.1	-13.0	-23.1	2.1
Reserves (change)	+7.7	+7.2	+12.9	+8.7	-7.9	+18.7	-26.2	-7.6	+10.5
Memorandum:									
Exports growth (%)	7.2	12.9	6.8	2.7	11.0	4.8	-10.8	-3.5	-15.6
Imports growth (%)	7.5	31.0	51.1	6.7	15.4	-2.0	-9.9	-6.2	-21.1
GDP growth (%)	1.8	5.9	4.2	2.8	3.7	1.3	-1.0	0.2	-1.0
Import penetration ratio[c]	8.5	10.9	15.6	16.4	19.2	n.a.	n.a.	20.5	n.a.
Export propensity[d]	13.2	13.7	14.0	14.5	n.a.	n.a.	n.a.	17.0	n.a.

[a] Annual averages.

[b] Figures are inflated by the debt exchange in the issuance of Brady bonds.

[c] Imports as percentage of supply (output less exports plus imports) in manufacturing.

[d] Exports as percentage of sales in manufacturing.

SOURCES: Depec-Banco Central do Brasil; UNCTAD (1997); and Moreira (1997).

crisis and subsequent closure of capital markets to Brazil. It is somewhat surprising that the adjustment strategy followed after 1982, and the instruments employed, far outlived the circumstances in which they were born. Autarky, or self-sufficiency, was openly advocated as import-penetration ratios fell to 4 percent or lower in the late 1980s, heralding what seemed to be the climax of import substitution, the long-awaited moment of economic independence.

By the early 1990s, however, these illusions were rapidly fading. As the debt crisis receded, Brazil started nurturing an acute sensation of having missed the globalization train, a feeling that was heightened by declining productivity growth, increasing distributive tensions, and hyperinflation. Yet, even though the promises of import substitution were not fulfilled, the constituencies for the preservation of the self-sufficiency model remained strong and loudly attached to Asian-style interventionist ideas of industrial policy. I shall not review the very complex political economy surrounding trade reform and the trade orientation of Brazilian development (see Fritsch and Franco, 1993), but it should be noted that a crucial moment in these discussions coincided with the Real Plan. The turn toward a current-account deficit shown in Table 3, reflecting the combined influence of trade reform, the new exchange-rate policy, and stabilization, was very rapid. Brazilian authorities would see this change largely as a return to normalcy: domestic investment in an emerging economy such as Brazil's should naturally be larger than savings. The question remaining was how much larger was ideal.

In the language of Figure 5, a movement southwest along the BP curve, with lower inflation and currency appreciation, would necessarily imply an increase in the current-account deficit. In that simple framework, there would be no consideration about whether the implied trajectory of indebtedness was too risky, or even unsustainable, from the point of view of an intertemporal capacity to pay. It might simply be that the low-inflation equilibrium pictured in the figure was beyond reach, or that it was feasible only under a very friendly international capital market or combined with a waiver of financing problems. How can we be sure?

There seems to be little precise guidance about the feasibility and implied risks of different options. The analysis of balance-of-payments (indebtedness) sustainability usually combines a number of elements on highly diversified scorecards of country-risk measures: ratios such as debt to gross domestic product (GDP) and debt servicing to exports; golden rules such as the one relating exports growth and effective interest rates to debt; as well as considerations about exchange-rate flexibility, savings and fiscal balance, investment and future output of tradable goods, and the banking system and politics. All these ingredients compose a rich menu from which rating agencies and other suppliers of sovereign-risk rankings customize their formulas. Inconsistencies among different rankings, not to mention the inability to forecast recent disasters, highlight the large degree of discretion involved in the country-risk industry, the performance of which has been quite poor in the last few years. The problem has many dimensions, indeed.

Gian Maria Ferretti and Assaf Razin (1996, p. 65), in a state-of-the-art discussion of current-account-sustainability indicators, conclude "that a specific threshold on persistent current-account deficits (such as 5 percent of GDP for three to four years) is not in itself a sufficiently informative indicator of sustainability." Following the Mexican experience in 1994, and without much scientific reasoning, figures of about 3 or 4 percent of GDP became benchmarks for the safety frontier for the current-account deficits,[24] even though a number of investment-graded countries could exhibit larger numbers. Later, with the Asian crisis and the turbulence following the Russian moratorium, certainties in this field were considerably reduced. Assessments became everywhere more conservative and even somewhat biased toward stressing vulnerabilities: the costs (commercial and reputational) of missing a large meltdown seemed higher than the "type II" mistake of forecasting a disaster that might not happen. In fact, the latter usually goes unnoticed.

In any event, current-account-deficit figures (as a percentage of GDP) remain a very popular, perhaps the most popular, indicator of sustainability, although they are qualified by broad perceptions about ongoing fundamental changes and, even more visibly, by other aspects of the balance of payments, such as the nature of the capital inflows affecting a given country. The Brazilian numbers in Table 3 show, for 1997 and 1998, current-account deficits slightly above 4 percent of GDP, but there were three extenuating circumstances. First, borrowing conditions had been steadily improving—maturity and spreads moved from an average of 3.9 years and 606 basis points in 1992–93 to 9.1 years and 395 basis points (over comparable U.S. Treasury securities) in 1997 (see registered-loan figures from the Banco Central do Brasil). Second, numbers for foreign direct investment (FDI), showed an unambiguous surge, rising from US$2.6 billion in 1994 to US$26.1 in 1998. As a percentage of global flows, FDI in Brazil seems slowly to be recovering the shares typical of the 1970s, that is, 5 percent of total world flows, a level more or less in line with Brazil's share in world-value-added in manufacturing. Privatizations have been responsible for approximately one-third of these observed flows. Since 1996, Brazil has been second only to China as an FDI host among emerging economies, and it is ranked sixth overall. Brazil's FDI was equivalent to 75 percent of the current account in 1998, up from 51 percent in 1997, and up from 41 percent in 1996. In the first quarter of 1999, this proportion reached 150 percent.

The third positive balance-of-payments development following the Real Plan was the large advance in the share of imports subject to financing. In the 1980s, imports typically had to be paid for in cash, but in the mid–1990s, and especially after Brazil's Brady bonds were issued, only 20 percent of imports were paid in cash (that is, within

[24] Cline (1997, p. 396), in his comment to Dornbusch, argues that "this kind of magnitude has considerable merit," because it would be just enough to stabilize external debt at, say, 40 percent of GDP when dollar prices grow by 3 percent a year and GDP grows by 5 percent.

thirty days of customs clearance). Of course, as Brazil has moved from cash to financing, there has been a considerable cash-flow effect favoring international reserves. It should also be noted that when imports are subject to direct financing, the underlying current-account deficit is "born," with a corresponding positive entry in the capital account, that is, the current-account deficit and borrowing occur simultaneously.

In the world before the Asian crisis, and especially before the Russian moratorium, all this seemed fine to an innocent bystander. Brazil was in a transition in which gradual expenditure switching (achieved through a slow exchange-rate crawl and high productivity growth) and reforms addressing savings capacity would allow increasingly large rates of growth under external balance, lower distributive tensions, and inflation at international levels. This transition was occurring while observers were debating whether Brazil had a problem with domestic savings, with competitiveness, or with both, and were discussing what would be the optimal combinations of expenditure reduction and switching, and of fundamental reforms, to address the situation. External constraints were obviously crucial in framing these decisions, and uncertainties in this area would have to be taken into consideration.

Combining Stabilization and Trade Reform

Arguments about medium-term sustainability notwithstanding, the very rapid evolution of the current account toward a significant deficit naturally raised concerns. A look at the details of Table 3, especially at the figures for growth rates and penetration ratios of imports suggests that the implementation of stabilization may be the key to understanding where the current account was headed. It would seem natural to accept the return of current-account deficits as normal following a stabilization. When trade reform is launched on top of a stabilization, however, the movement toward a current-account deficit may be much stronger and much less predictable.

One knows, from the accepted wisdom on liberalization episodes following the pioneer work of Jagdish Bhagwati (1978) and Anne Krueger (1978) in the late 1970s, that import liberalization would need a devaluation in order to maintain the trade surplus (deficit) at existing levels. The devaluation would offset perfectly the removal of tariffs *cum* subsidies existing in the previously distorted equilibrium, and its impact would be felt mostly on resource allocation, not (necessarily) on the macroeconomy, which is presumed to be in external balance at the

31

onset of the reform. Yet, it was forcefully argued that Brazil was initiating import liberalization with a gigantic trade surplus and with what was seen as an undervalued exchange rate. A 1994 World Bank report would note that "compared to other Latin American countries, Brazil was [early in 1994] the only one that has not seen a sizable appreciation in its real exchange rate in the 1990s, when foreign capital inflows into the Latin American region exploded in size" (World Bank, 1994, p. 64; see also Calvo, Leiderman, and Reinhart, 1993, p. 118). In addition, sharp increases in productivity, especially after 1990, greatly increased competitiveness. In the presence of sluggish GDP per capita growth, this would mean that productivity in the tradable-goods sector was growing much more rapidly than in the nontradable sectors. "Typically," the World Bank report continues (p. 66), "this would result in an appreciation of the real exchange rate especially since the increase in productivity has been much higher than in the developed countries which are Brazil's main trading partners." The increase in productivity and surge in capital inflows were entirely absorbed in increases in international reserves; as the report notes (p. 69), "a strategy of reserve accumulation to offset a real appreciation warranted by market fundamentals can be very expensive," given sterilization costs, which are estimated (p. 70) at 0.5 percent of GDP a year. This description appears to fit very well the model developed by Calvo, Reinhart, and Végh (1994).

The alleged necessity of an offsetting devaluation in cases of trade reform reveals a potential conflict of interest with stabilization policy, to the extent that the latter requires, or naturally produces, exchange-rate appreciation. A recent World Bank manual on trade reforms would argue that "an important source of tension between stabilization and liberalization programs is that successful trade liberalization must be supported by a real depreciation, while disinflation can result in an appreciation of the real exchange rate" (Thomas and Nash, 1991, p. 102). How, exactly, should policymakers behave when simultaneously conducting both stabilization and trade liberalization programs? Should these programs be conducted simultaneously? What should be their optimal timing? How much weight should be given to initial conditions?

Textbook advice on trade reform considers the simultaneity of stabilization and trade liberalization to be dangerous and suggests that it be avoided outright (Thomas and Nash, 1991, p. 103). Observers more skeptical about the impacts of trade reform, seeing weaknesses both in theoretical justifications and in hard evidence of gains in specific episodes, tend to approach the tension between liberalization and

32

stabilization with much more pragmatism.[25] Others, such as Bruno (1993), recalling the Eastern European transition countries, for which resource misallocation seemed obvious and huge, would sharply oppose the textbook recommendation and favor instead a "big push" approach, seemingly admitting increasing returns from economic reforms. Yet, what seems to be crucial to the specific policy decision faced by Brazilians is an assessment of the potential gains to be made from further liberalization and a judgment about the magnitude of existing distortions and the progress achieved by the trade-reform measures taken since 1990. These gains would have to be weighed against the tensions that liberalization would introduce into the stabilization program.

The decision in Brazil in 1994 was to continue both programs, because policymakers had difficulties segregating stabilization from reforms. Hyperinflation and fiscal disarray, on the one hand, and the accumulation of distortions in trade and industrial policies, on the other, seemed to be different halves of the same process of policy deterioration, "a process of predatory privatization of the state," with fiscal and regulatory expressions that could not be attacked in isolation (Fritsch and Franco, 1993, p. 36). For this reason, policymakers were convinced that stabilization and trade reform would benefit one another by creating a powerful inducement for change: liberalization would change market structures, thereby increasing contestability of markets, exposing local oligopolies to competition, allowing the dismantling of the price-control machinery, and hitting at the very heart of the import-substitution culture.[26] There was no question that it would help the cause of stabilization both immediately and also through its long-run impacts in the form of higher rates of productivity growth. Nevertheless, the extended planning horizons allowed by price stability, as well as the better visibility of the undistorted price system, would help considerably the investment and restructuring decisions following liberalization. In addition, programs such as privatizations and concessions would, apart

[25] On general grounds, one should be careful "not to oversell trade reform as a cure-all for economic problems" (Rodrik, 1992, p. 103), because it should be seen much more as an "enabling environment" than as something to secure prosperity. According to Krugman (1995, p. 33), "the widespread belief that moving to free trade and free markets will produce a dramatic acceleration in developing countries' growth represents a leap of faith, rather than a conclusion based on hard evidence."

[26] The benefits of combining stabilization with trade liberalization should not be taken as a general proposition, as Rodrik (1992, p. 98) points out with reference to Chile. Yet, there was no question in Brazil that this combination would be crucial in the Brazilian case.

from their fiscal impacts, greatly enhance efficiency, generating price and technological externalities. There seemed to be important gains in having these reforms reinforcing each other in the right direction and in signaling an entirely new development model to be constructed out of successive waves of productivity improvement. "Big push" arguments, commonly used for transition economies, were certainly in order in Brazil.

The Initial Move

The Brazilian exchange-rate regime would have to be designed to face the challenges of both the stabilization and trade-reform (structural-reform) agendas, and timing and flexibility would be crucial. Also crucial would be a well-defined strategy, in which a number of considerations would be important. The first such consideration was that the magnitude of change potentially derived from the combination of stabilization with trade and industrial-policy reform was nothing less than monumental. This should not be seen as an argument for a preemptive devaluation, which would do considerable, and possibly deadly, damage to stabilization but, rather, as an argument for the preservation of degrees of freedom to face unforeseen developments as the program unfolded. Even though a devaluation could always be presented as a cure-all prescription, to privilege external balance to the total detriment of internal balance (or of nominal targets) during the crucial moments of the struggle against hyperinflation was an impractical plan, at least while the indexation devices were set at full alert. Besides, faith in the progress of fiscal policy and in reforms more generally, and the perception that the international financial atmosphere was friendly, helped cool devaluation ideas.

A second consideration was that stabilization would have its decisive battle in the first few months, whereas trade reform and its implications would be felt through time. The importance of inflation results at the onset of the program could hardly be overemphasized, given Brazilians' propensity for indexation and the traumas suffered from unsuccessful stabilization plans in the past. Defensive behavior against a possible failure could severely endanger an otherwise sound effort. Credibility was crucial and would be measured by results. Inflation numbers for the first few months would therefore have to be convincing. In addition, and most important, it would have been virtually impossible to persuade the Brazilian Congress to accept the annualization of all indexation had the first few months' inflation been high.

34

A third consideration was that the URV experiment had resulted in a strong coordination of pricing and wage decisions, at the cost of hyperindexation, which to some extent strengthened the connection of the real to the dollar, a new development in Brazil. Even though the coordination helped stop the rise in the nominal price level, the dollarization link introduced a new danger into a process in which the key element was the elimination of indexation (the nominalization) of all prices (see Bacha, 1998). These developments would no doubt greatly amplify the impact of exchange-rate movements, because a nominal devaluation could be both neutral and highly inflationary in an indexation-prone environment. The impacts might be asymmetric, or an appreciation might have only a limited effect on prices but a considerable effect on de-dollarization.

A fourth consideration was the president's unwillingness (in addition to very concrete political obstacles) to consider the idea of a currency board, an option that had a number of supporters. One explanation for his reluctance is that the path from the old to the new equilibrium (from A to C in Figure 5) would, perhaps, be too slow, the movement being produced solely by inflation, with too much chance given for indexation to reappear and reinstate the inflationary spiral. The uncertainty about the extent of this residual inflation would make the fixing of a given exchange rate a risky proposition. Other explanations were his unwillingness to surrender the idea of a national currency and the hardly disputable assertion that Brazil had not experienced the degree of monetary and financial decadence that one saw in, for instance, Argentina. There was no alternative to a currency board in Argentina, given the spontaneous advance of dollarization (an expression of which was the small difference between narrow and broad definitions of money—M1 and M4—at the end of the hyperinflation cycle.[27] In Argentina, financial wealth had been mostly shifted abroad, but in Brazil, capital flight was not particularly significant. The presence of a large M4 (mostly public debt), as compared to M1, raises a number of difficult questions about the level of reserves that are needed to set the arrangement. It was not unlikely that available reserves would be insufficient. Besides, some experts thought that a compulsory restructuring of the domestic debt would be needed, and this was entirely out of the question.

[27] M1 is the sum of all circulating coins, paper money, and checkable deposits at banks and savings institutions; M4 is M1 plus savings and time deposits as well as liquid financial assets of several kinds.

With all this in mind, the decision was made simply to start with a float. It would be the first time since the abandonment of the gold standard in 1931 that a country functioning under exchange controls had allowed the exchange rate to be freely determined in the market place.[28] Supply and demand would govern one of the crucial prices in the economy and would issue a clean statement on the quality of the newly created currency. The result was little different than expected. Given the high levels of confidence, and of interest rates, the real appreciated, much to the surprise of the man on the street and the media, who were impressed by the fact the real was worth "more than a dollar."[29] Irrelevant as it may sound, a nominal fall in the exchange rate served as a signal for the, as yet unseen, price deflation being experienced in many other markets. Nothing like that had ever been witnessed. In contrast to other stabilization episodes in Brazil, the law of supply and demand was on the government's side this time and *it was working*—even with respect to the dollar! Expectations about the success of the new plan were at their highest point, while deflation, as intended, destroyed formal and informal indexation rules. The stabilization program was off to a good start.

Thanks to the impetus given by these developments, the initial success of the Real Plan went far beyond the highest expectations. Even though inflation, as measured by price indices, showed numbers that evoked mixed responses—such as the numbers seen in Table 1 for the "clean" indices—the program's impact was mostly monitored by the daily readings of "point-to-point" indices[30] (such as the popular basic food-basket index) released by a unions-funded research institute.[31] These showed a continuous deflation for July (–4.4 percent) and August (–4.3 percent).[32]

Yet, as already mentioned, one of the most difficult aspects of a stabilization plan is dealing with its own success, especially when the

[28] The brief experience in March and April of 1990 was too clouded by the simultaneously implemented asset freeze to be meaningful as a departure from an exchange-rate regime.

[29] During the four months prior to the introduction of the new currency, exchange rates between the Cruzeiro real and the dollar kept the dollar at approximately 96 cents of the URV. The float would bring this number down to 83 cents (see Figure 6 below).

[30] Point-to-point variations of price levels are changes computed without averaging.

[31] A cost of living index, known as "Cesta Básica" and mostly based on foodstuffs, is released daily as a joint effort of the unions' research institute (Dieese) and regional consumer-defense organizations (Procons).

[32] In URV terms, the basic basket index rose 10.4 percent in June, clearly revealing the presence of some price overshooting just before the issuance of the new currency in July.

game is only in the beginning and the bad news, in the form of the enabling fundamentals, is all in the future. It is important to preserve flexibility within the exchange-rate regime to allow for the reversal of appreciation, and possibly a slide toward depreciation, as the effects of trade liberalization start to be felt more significantly or if the current-account deficit appears too large. In Brazil, full priority was given to stabilization at the onset of the program, but it was known that the next chapter of the Real Plan, which would be marked by structural change and preparations for growth resumption, would most likely require a new stance or a new foreign-exchange regime. What should be the next step? Why not simply continue with the float? What would be the most appropriate regime for this second stage of the stabilization plan?

The Development of the Crawling-Bands Regime

The choice of a European-style target-zone system, or a bands system, was a compromise between the newly discovered virtues of market forces in determining the exchange rate, the concern with new phenomena such as capital surges, "hot money," and derivatives (most likely introducing the perils of excessive volatility), and the old constraints to market mechanisms derived from the prolonged exposure to exchange controls. It can also be explained, by analogy with the experiences of Chile, Israel, and Mexico, as a system meant to combine concerns with competitiveness (or the will to improve it) and the convenience of counting on nominal-exchange-rate flexibility to respond to internal and external shocks, this being "a common feature of the aftermath of several important heterodox stabilizations" and thus the essence of a "new breed of exchange rate bands" (Cukierman, Kiguel and Liviatan, 1994, p. 260). John Williamson (1999, pp. 1–2) strongly advocates the crawling-band regime, as opposed to flexible exchange rates, on a more general basis, given "the obvious and extreme lack of the sort of stabilizing speculation that theory says one has to rely on to stabilize a floating exchange rate regime," or "the evidence that asset markets in general, and foreign exchange in particular, are driven by herd behavior rather than rational expectations." Maurice Obstfeld (1995) and others cite the European experience in order to raise skepticism about the working of target zones, and majority opinion seems to be moving toward the idea that emerging economies should adopt either a free float or a currency board. I shall return to this issue later in the essay.

Despite the well-crafted *ex post* reasoning, it is more interesting to observe that the Brazilian target zones and their variations developed as natural byproducts of the central bank's reactions to market excesses.

37

At first, the central bank bought reserves over the counter, but it was unable to stop the real's appreciation. It continued to buy until September 1994, when the exchange rate reached its lowest admissible level, the floor unofficially fixed by the central bank at R$0.83 to the dollar. Next, as the exchange rate started to depreciate too quickly, in response to the Mexican crisis at the end of 1994, the central bank sold reserves at R$0.86 to the dollar. The R$0.83 floor was established to avoid excessive appreciation; the R$0.86 ceiling was meant to prevent depreciation, which could, at that time, have endangered stabilization. When these limits were made official, in March 1995, the central bank fixed new (higher) bands, at R$0.88 and R$0.93 to the dollar. These bands have been changing, more or less annually, up to the levels seen in Figure 6, even though the development of systematic interventions inside the bands has diminished their importance over time. The broad bands seen in Figure 6 remained relevant as signaling devices and remained at R$1.12 and R$1.22 to the dollar until January 1999, when the regime was changed back to a float.

The picture shown in Figure 6 is no different from that seen in many other countries, that is, bands that have been pulled up from time to time and, in certain countries, have given way to crawling bands, or corridors, explicitly merging the wisdom on target zones (or the lessons of European experience) with the Latin American tradition of exchange-rate indexation (crawling pegs). Figure 6 shows the impact of the initial float, some volatility within the R$0.88 and R$0.93 band enforced from April to July 1995, and then, a very well behaved trajectory of the market rate within the bands, which is explained by the strength of intraband interventions. In this respect, the Brazilian experience is no different from the experiences of Chile, Israel, and Mexico, for instance, where the central banks all intervened around central parities to prevent volatility. What seems distinctively Brazilian is the intervention technology, known as "spread auctions" or "double auctions," regularly deployed along with regular buy or sell auctions. This technology consists in the central bank's mimicking the behavior of a trader asking for spreads in the market place while simultaneously working with all the leading foreign-exchange-dealer institutions, which are obliged to submit bid and ask prices for foreign exchange, with the maximum spreads and minimum amounts tendered being fixed by the central bank. This system reduces the dispersion of quotes to a minimum and is specifically designed to allow for a quiet transition from one target zone to another, which is unquestionably the most delicate part of any policy of exchange-rate bands involving infrequent realignments in

FIGURE 6

CRAWLING BANDS

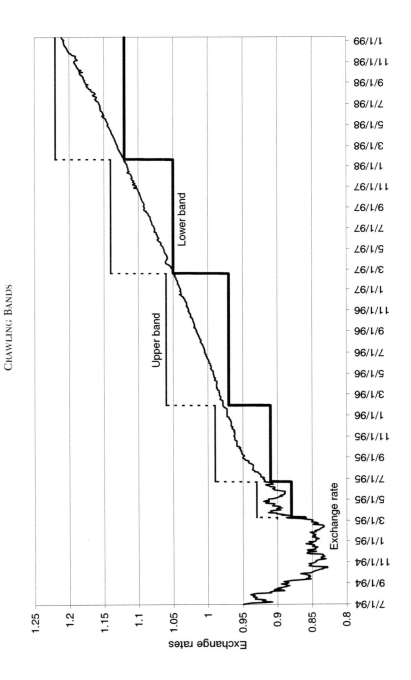

intervention points. When this new auction system was introduced in June 1995, and for a considerable time afterward, bid-ask spreads were so large that it was common for the central bank to buy *and* sell dollars in the same spread auction. In 1995, sixty spread auctions were called, with US$5.1 billion bought and US$3.6 billion sold. In 1996, eighty-six spread auctions yielded US$2.5 billion bought and US$3.3 billion sold, and in 1997, seventy-five auctions yielded US$603 million bought and US$224 million sold.[33]

As it happened, the bid-ask spreads implicit in these auctions started to be enlarged and assumed the character of an inner band, while bid-ask spreads in the market narrowed to the fourth decimal. Although these inner bands were much narrower than the larger ones, they were much more important for the market as indications of the central bank's desires. These "minibands" as they became known, had also an upward slope, because the ceiling and floor were both readjusted in small steps during the month at rates of between 0.5 percent and 0.65 percent (equivalent to annual rates of 6.1 percent and 7.5 percent). They might well be described as "crawling minibands," and because the higher rate applied to the ceiling, the minibands were slowly enlarged, the expectation being of a miniband with a 3 to 4 percent width after a couple of years. The regime was indeed approaching something very similar to the Chilean regime.

The Convertibility Regime and the Limits of Intervention

Beyond the ingenuity of the system itself, what seems remarkable, in light of international experience, was the Brazilian central bank's ability to force "rules of the game," binding as these were, on the foreign-exchange market. It is useful, in this connection, to draw attention to some key aspects of the Brazilian exchange-rate regulations, or "arrangements," to use the IMF's terminology. Technically, Brazil operates under exchange-rate controls and has done so for a long time. Since 1933, for example, exporters have had to surrender the hard currency they earn to the central bank or to sell it, as authorized by the central bank, in the Brazilian foreign-exchange market. In addition, since legislation on "foreign capital" was enacted in the 1960s (Law 4,131/62), its basic principles have changed very little: all capital inflows—loans, FDI, portfolio—have to be registered (thus, authorized), and repatriations can

---

[33] The puzzling question is how the central bank could intervene this way in a market that had all the credentials to qualify it as efficient. The issue here is volatility, or a degree of dispersion of expectations that in no way should be seen as inefficient.

be made only up to the original inflow. Thus, capital outflows are nearly always limited to previous inflows, there being no convertibility of local savings into dollars, except in very specific windows during which the central bank exercises a considerable degree of surveillance and suasion. In fact, Brazil is not even an Article VIII country.[34]

Payments on account of interest have to obey conditions set at the moment of the loan registration, there being no room for changes and anticipations. Dividends, to be remitted, require the company to undertake specific balance-sheet and profit-and-loss demonstrations and to pay taxes due; only after these steps have been duly certified, may banks sell the foreign exchange for the remittance.

It is true that these rigidities have created problems through the years. The strategy to deal with them, however, was not outright deregulation, but the creation of specific windows through which certain types of transactions could flow on a fast track. Indeed, registration may be a purely statistical step, as, for instance, in the case of portfolio investment under the so-called "Annex IV," for which all registration and control of repatriations is made on a real-time basis, offering no obstacle to the quick movements typical of such markets.[35] The fast-track approach also applies to sundry items within services that conduct moderate-size transactions in the floating-rate market. In other cases, registration assumes the character of an authorization, because it is granted only with conditions, for instance, with minimum tenures for loans.

For all these reasons, there are no significant holdings of reals offshore, even in neighboring countries, and all trading against foreign currencies takes place within Brazil, with the central bank playing the roles of both regulator and clearinghouse.[36] Indeed, this is the one

---

[34] The obstacles to Brazil's compliance with Article VIII of the IMF's Articles of Agreement were mostly in the form of taxes levied on foreign exchange bought for the import of services and the existence of a second market for foreign exchange designed to absorb transactions previously taking place in the black market. Both obstacles have been removed, so that Brazil is now ready to declare compliance.

[35] Annexes I through V of Resolution 1289 of Conselho Monetario Nacional (CMN) regulate all vehicles for foreign portfolio investment into Brazil. Annex IV is the most popular of these vehicles.

[36] The Chicago Mercantile Exchange (CME) trades futures contracts denominated in reals, though in a nondeliverable form and in small volumes. Nearly all foreign-exchange trading in reals—both primary and interbank—takes place through online contracts entered within the Sistema de Informações do Banco Central (SISBACEN), the central bank's multipurpose network to which all financial institutions in Brazil are connected. Gradual

key institutional feature that confers added power to intervention, and it becomes especially relevant because the effectiveness of intervention is closely related to the sustainability of a given exchange-rate regime, and also to its vulnerability to attacks. The fact that the real is not an internationally traded currency surely restricts the possibilities in this connection. Simply put, there is little room for shortening the real from abroad, because there are practically no reals abroad for sellers to deliver, making short-squeezing considerably easier. Other things being equal, intervention seems more effective (if it does not deviate from fundamentals) in inconvertible currencies, for which pressures cannot go much beyond the balance-of-payments flow, than in Group of Seven (G–7) currencies, for which the effectiveness of intervention has to be assessed in relation to asset markets on both sides of the frontier, where stock equilibria may shift, moving funds in very large amounts. Inconvertibility is therefore an important institutional feature of Brazil's foreign-exchange market, as the pressures produced by the Asian crisis and the turbulence following the Russian moratorium aptly demonstrate.

6 Responses to the Asian Crisis

The Asian crisis represents a watershed in the thinking on exchange-rate regimes, capital flows, and crisis management in emerging economies. This section considers the Brazilian response to the Asian crisis in connection with two issues. First, it discusses the issue of prevention, or the fact that different responses to capital surges may significantly affect a given economy's vulnerability when the moment comes for the reversal of such flows. It is known that, other things being equal, capital mobility reduces the macroeconomic options available to any open economy that is left to choose between an independent monetary policy and a fixed exchange rate, a choice that is only more difficult if fiscal policy is unsuitable. The issue considered here, however, is the extent to which controls and restrictions to capital inflows may loosen this trade-off and whether the methods available to manage the capital account can help avoid excessive exposure to external events in general and to the Asian

---

foreign-exchange deregulation over the years destroyed the parallel market, mostly by creating a special section in the foreign-exchange market that had lower levels of documentation designed initially for tourism dollars. This special section, known as "mercado flutuante," broadened its base so that the parallel market was left solely with cash transactions, largely crime related, and mostly on the Paraguayan frontier. Early in 1999, all barriers between this market and the mainstream foreign-exchange market were removed.

crisis in particular. Has Brazil done enough to reduce its vulnerability? What is the optimal approach to increased capital mobility and capital-account convertibility in times of globalization?

The second issue considered is the fact that the contagion from Asia came through brand new vehicles, such as the markets for Brady bonds and the stock exchange. The authorities considered that the more adverse external environment would not change the nature of Brazil's stabilization and reform agenda but that it definitely changed the urgency with which things should be done. The monetary tightening, the fiscal effort, the relaxation of restrictions to inflows of capital, and the intervention in the derivatives exchanges were a successful response to the crisis,[37] even though the nondelivery of crucial parts of this effort proved to be a serious problem later, by the time of the Russian moratorium.

Some key institutional features of an economy such as Brazil's, which acts under currency inconvertibility, are important for defining the ways through which attacks may be generated. The domestic public debt has been an important element in this process, there being a clear connection between the exchange rate and the fiscal stance. Foreign-exchange derivatives have also been an important and peculiar ingredient in the financial turbulence experienced by Brazil during the last few years. Their development in the economy has been nothing less than phenomenal, and their implications for the conduct of policies implying intervention in the spot market are far from trivial

Capital Surges and Their Effects

The issues raised by capital surges are very old: whether to abstain from or to take advantage of the opportunities offered by a friendly international environment, especially when it involves capital flows that are bound to disappear on short notice. Many times in the history of Latin American economies, there have been long spells during which cheap foreign capital, often involving push and pull factors, has offered sometimes irresistible incentives toward incurring large current-account deficits. These have almost invariably ended in drastic reversals and painful rescheduling exercises and devaluations.

---

[37] A family of issues not entirely related to this essay's terms of reference concerns the parallels between Brazil and Asia—namely, the features of Asian economies presumably responsible for the Asian problems that can also be found in Brazil. The involvement of the Brazilian state in banking and in the debate on active industrial policies are interesting themes that are not discussed in this essay.

From the late 1980s onward, as the acute moments of the 1982 debt crisis were left behind, capital flows to emerging economies began to gain strength. These flows were initially selective, coming to areas least affected by the crisis. They included more and more recipients, however, as the number of Brady-bond countries increased, as the secondary market for Brady bonds facilitated borrowing, and as the transition economies joined the group of emerging markets tapping into international capital markets. The origins of the huge flows to the emerging economies in the 1990s have been extensively studied, and the conclusions have been constantly revised in connection with the crises that began in 1995 with the Mexican debacle (see Eichengreen and Fishlow, 1998). Most frequently, crises seem to start from a capital surge occurring a few years before the event. The question of how emerging economies should deal with capital surges has a lot to do with being vulnerable to a crisis.

In the 1990s, there were many cases of emerging economies in which foreign investments entering the country were very large in proportion to exports or GDP, creating the macroeconomic problems typical of an abundance of foreign exchange. The ability of the emerging economies to use macroeconomic policy and capital-account management to defend themselves against such capital surges had been discussed, although without a sense of urgency. Capital bonanzas are basically good news; they are often significant stimuli to economic development. If they might create problems in the future, it is natural to defer concern. The sample of countries subject to strong interest on the part of foreign investors displays a combination of factors that include exchange-rate appreciation, sterilized intervention (with accumulation of reserves), selective incentives to outflows, liberalization in trade and services, increased reserve requirements on banks' foreign liabilities, and taxes or direct controls on capital inflows. These were all accepted as commendable by investors and analysts, including restrictions on inflows, up to a point (see Calvo, Leiderman, and Reinhart, 1993; Corbo and Hernandez, 1996; Lee, 1996; and Polak, 1998). Studies do recognize, however, that the effectiveness of all these defenses grows weaker as inflows grow stronger and last longer. Appreciation and current-account deficits may become too large and too difficult to avoid. Emerging economies may be overwhelmed by this financial variety of "Dutch disease," which seems even worse than the traditional version produced by commodities bonanzas, because it induces large current-account deficits that are not as easily reversible as the capital inflows that caused them. Emerging economies might be given too much

44

incentive to enter into dangerous trajectories of indebtedness and, in some cases, might be encouraged by the belief (warranted or not) that bailouts will be available in the event of unfavorable developments.

Brazil was a latecomer in the capital-flow bonanza that began in the mid–1980s. While many other emerging economies were fighting to stop excessive appreciation and to contain current-account deficits in the early 1990s, Brazil, which was consumed by hyperinflation, was at least temporarily disqualified from joining the party. Capital inflows started to be a concern for Brazilian authorities in 1993, when the first movements toward the Real Plan were being prepared. There had been no exchange-rate appreciation up to this point; the current account was in surplus (see Table 3), and international reserves had grown from US$9.4 billion at the end of 1991 to US$32.2 billion at the end of 1993. Since then, Brazil had needed to consider policies to defend itself from a capital surge but had done so in the context of a long-awaited stabilization effort. It was only in the second half of 1993 that Brazil started to restrict some kinds of capital inflows, notably, fixed-income investments flowing through the Annex IV provision.

The kinds of restrictions practiced in Brazil at this time benefited from the previously built exchange-control machinery that had been developed, in an entirely different context, to prevent outflows. Given that all inflows require an authorization, the central bank has, for quite some time, been defining specific windows for certain transactions in the capital account and has been imposing selective treatment as regards documentation, conditions, and restrictions. There have been minimum-tenure requirements for borrowing abroad, varying from six months to three years; fiscal advantages for long maturities (that is, income-tax exemption for interest payments of loans longer than ninety-six months); and restrictions to excessively high interest rates. Interest-equalization taxes have also been used, especially for short-term fixed-income inflows, and even (for a while) for portfolio investment, at rates that have climbed as high as 7 percent. There are also restrictions to leads and lags in export advances and import financing, respectively, aimed at the short-term inflows generated.

The intensity of these restrictions varied considerably according to the circumstances. A recent study has even shown that the restrictions displayed a considerable degree of endogeneity—that is, a statistical measure of controls would exhibit increases during booms and reductions during times of distress (Cardoso and Goldfajn, 1998). Indeed, restrictions were kept somewhat narrow during the period following the Mexican crisis, because the crisis was thought to be having little

45

impact on Brazil and capital inflows continued to be strong in response to still-high interest rates and to the growing perception that the Brazilian stabilization was a success. Over time, as interest rates fell and long-term capital, typically FDI, entered Brazil in larger and larger amounts, restrictions to short-term capital were tightened, producing a displacement effect on inflows into Brazil. From September 1995 to September 1997, outflows of short-term capital through the floating-rate window may have reached US$25 billion, through the combination of lower interest-rate differentials and the continuing 2 percent taxation on inflows.[38] Meanwhile, the impressive increase in FDI, portfolio investment, and long-term borrowing (subject still to a three-year minimum maturity) prevented any significant alteration in international reserves. Thanks to this stance, Brazil would slowly rid itself of the short-term inflows that had entered the country in response to interest-rate increases following the Mexican crisis and would be ready to face the Asian crisis with a much lower stock of volatile foreign capital parked in short-term fixed-income instruments. This improvement in the quality of the foreign capital entering Brazil, and in the solidity of reserves, significantly reduced the economy's vulnerability to unfavorable market conditions. Indeed, this was a good argument against the claim that controls were ineffective against capital inflows,[39] but it did not prevent the authorities from understanding the limitations of such instruments. The controls were certainly helpful as a secondary support to policies to defend against surges, or to deal with crises, but they should never be assigned a more ambitious role.

Even while emerging-market countries were implementing new kinds of controls over inflows, the industrial countries were firmly engaged in efforts to liberalize capital flows. There have been extensive debates within the framework of multilateral organizations about FDI (in, for

[38] As discussed above, the floating-rate market was originally the segment of the mainstream market designed to attract transactions away from the black market. As it turned out, in the mid–1990s, it became a window for short-term inflows that was controlled by heavy surveillance and suasion and by an interest-equalization tax at entry. Even though this market was not subject formally to the principle that outflows may not exceed previous inflows, the central bank could enforce the principle on an informal basis.

[39] In statistical tests of the effectiveness of restrictions on capital inflows into Brazil, an argument was made that they merely caused a change in the composition of inflows. Yet, one may say there was a very important change in the composition of inflows by virtue of controls and restrictions. This is exactly the point and the reason why the conclusion of ineffectiveness is unwarranted (see Reinhart and Smith, 1997; Cardoso and Goldfajn, 1998; and Garcia and Barcinski, 1998).

instance, the Multilateral Agreement on Investments) and about whether or not to give a mandate to the IMF to promote capital-account convertibility. This latter issue was presented at the October 1997 meeting of the IMF and World Bank in Hong Kong, at a time when the Asian crisis, although still in an early stage of development, was looming large on the horizon. It did not take long for the crisis to worsen and to show that the proposal was entirely inappropriate. It is notable that in 1994, the IMF had protested against the measures taken in Brazil to restrict capital inflows but that in 1997, that stance was praised. The issue of capital-account convertibility may simply have been a byproduct of an internal agenda crisis at the IMF.

Crisis and Response

The Asian crisis was not Brazil's first exposure to the dark side of financial globalization. The new features of this challenge, however, were, first, its origin (Mexico had been the source of trouble in the past) and, second, the vehicles of transmission. Shock waves from Asia came through markets that had become much more international over time, such as the stock exchanges, and from markets that were born offshore, such as the Brady-bond markets. New and fluid lines of transmission for foreign financial disturbances were also in operation. These combined a number of elements. Shortly before the crisis, it was common to see mutual funds using financing from international banks to hold Brazilian Brady bonds and stocks on a highly leveraged basis. These mutual funds included not only dedicated hedge funds and Brazilian funds offshore, but also nondedicated, presumably conservative, investments such as pension funds of all origins. The whole thing appeared risky, but the funds were either located offshore, or were not entirely visible, or relevant, to regulators.

As the crisis broke, and prices of emerging-market bonds and stocks collapsed, severe margin calls and much tougher "haircuts" were imposed by the banks financing these highly leveraged long positions in Brazilian stocks and Brady bonds. In this context of stricter liquidity abroad and much higher yields on Brady bonds, there was a strong pressure to sell, which was accompanied by collapsing prices and, by consequence, heavy losses, particularly in mutual funds. It was fortunate that the risky activity of carrying leveraged positions in emerging-market paper was essentially off balance sheet and segregated in mutual funds. The fact that the liability structure of mutual funds is much simpler than that of banks, and that Brazilian banks were involved in this market mostly indirectly through the sponsorship of

47

these funds, helped to deliver fund losses to the ultimate capitalists, without significant repercussions for the banks.[40] Indeed, although the balance sheets of Brazilian banks showed losses in the second-semester returns, these were entirely manageable. Foreign-exchange remittances from Brazil were necessary to make up for losses abroad, and these remittances put some pressure on the exchange rate, but the pressures produced by the collapse of Brady-bond prices were much more significant in view of the opportunities for arbitrage against domestic government debt instruments using Brady bonds and the paralysis in primary issuance of new debt instruments.

The extent and duration of the crisis, as well as its international repercussions, were difficult to ascertain as currency collapses and turmoil involved one country after the other in Asia. Fears of a world-wide crisis started to be seen here and there. From the standpoint of the Brazilian policies combining stabilization and reform, and the by no means unchallenged need to address serious structural issues, a major change in the international environment was clearly a matter of utmost concern. At the time, the responses available to Brazil were assessed on a more fundamental level, with reference to primary attitudes toward globalization. Should Brazil design its economic policy to address an upcoming world financial collapse and a global glut, from which Brazil should do nothing but shelter itself by returning to autarkic policies? Or should it think of the future as, according to the old cliché, bringing challenges and opportunities?

It seemed sensible to presume neither the end of the world nor an overly optimistic view that the crisis would be short-lived and, if restricted to the region, might even benefit other emerging economies. Temporary shocks may require nothing more than temporary defenses, mostly in the form of monetary tightening. Disturbances that have more lasting impacts may need more fundamental responses. Indica-tions were that the Asian crisis would produce a lasting shock, so that it was clearly advantageous to policymakers to seize the opportunity to press for significant reforms, that is, to introduce immediately fiscal measures that would otherwise have been taken in the future and at a slower pace. The implied philosophy was that the Brazilian government understood that the policies associated with the Real Plan were correct and that the change in the international landscape should produce only more urgency and speed in advancing the existing stabilization *cum*

[40] There remained, of course, the difficult issue of mutual funds that had negative net worth and were organized as limited-liability companies. Defaults were inevitable in such cases but fortunately had little visible impact.

reform agenda. The message in this response was that policymakers would be willing to sacrifice a couple of points in GDP growth in order to consolidate a transition toward a stronger economy along the lines that had been implicit in the Real Plan since the beginning. The option was for consistency, thus for a response with a strong fiscal component. Carried out in a credible way, a crowding-in process could even prevent significant losses in GDP growth: if fiscal fundamentals were improved on a permanent basis, the lowering of interest rates could be faster and deeper, most likely attracting additional private investment to take up the slack.

This philosophy conveyed a clear judgment about the relative importance of expenditure reduction and switching that finds justification in the fact that, with an end-of-the-year public-sector borrowing requirement (PSBR) at 6.1 percent of GDP in 1997, it would seem pointless to engage in expenditure switching in order to evade the attack on what was always clearly seen as the key issue, the fiscal imbalance. In addressing the fiscal deficit, moreover, one would not need much help from the exchange rate, given the slow devaluation built into the policies in place. For the vast majority of analysts, the fiscal issue was, and continues to be, the essence of the sustainability problem faced by Brazil, and it would not be any easier if the exchange-rate regime were changed. This would become clear later, in 1999.

In light of all this, the key aspects of the Brazilian response to pressures generated by the Asian events were a R$20 billion (about 2 percent of GDP) fiscal effort, which was approved in the Congress in a matter of weeks after the peak of the turbulence, and the doubling of interest rates to 3.03 percent a month (approximately 43 percent a year) in November 1997, a rise that was accompanied by indications of a trajectory of declining rates at an uncertain speed. Nothing was changed with regard to exchange-rate policy or the basic vision that the structural change under way (privatization, trade liberalization, productivity growth) would turn Brazil into a much stronger and competitive economy in the future. In this context, the relaxation of restrictions to short-term inflows—which was meant to be seen as temporary—helped international reserves to recover much faster than they otherwise would; this allowed the central bank to reduce interest rates faster as well.[41]

[41] With the deterioration in international borrowing conditions, the central bank reduced the minimum tenure for borrowing abroad to one year, and, in cases of renewal, to six months. These conditions, which would be available only temporarily (for authorizations given up to March 1, 1998), produced a flurry of inflows during the

There were substantial reserve losses in the last two months of 1997—the level falling from US$61.9 billion in September to US$52 billion in November—but the recovery was quick and strong. April's position reached US$74.6 billion, when basic interest rates were about 23 percent per year, that is, very close to the precrisis levels of 21.5 percent (see Figure 7).

It was true that most of the capital that was entering the country and increasing the reserves at this time was short term in nature. It was expected, however, that over time, the projected declines in domestic interest rates would encourage the same process of displacement in favor of longer-term inflows that had occurred after the Mexican crisis. There was little change in the trends in FDI, which continued to grow significantly. The anticipated privatization of the Brazilian telecom giant Telebrás, moreover, which occurred in the second quarter of 1998, only added to the idea that long-term capital would return to Brazil very soon. It seemed that Brazil would defeat the Asian illness, thanks to what was seen as a courageous response to fundamental weaknesses in the economy. Later, however, one would see the flaws in this response, and the price to pay for them would be very high.

Attacks and Defenses: Old and New Issues

The Asian events revealed many new opportunities for financial turbulence within a framework of globalized and highly leveraged markets affected by complex new derivative instruments and hedge funds, sometimes based in jurisdictions lacking high standards of prudential regulation and risk transparency. To say there is more capital mobility now than ever before seems an understatement, considering the wide consequences of these developments. But do these developments really create new conditions for currency attacks? And how vulnerable to an attack has Brazil become by virtue of these new conditions?

The issue of possible currency attacks in Brazil has been discussed since at least 1988, when the economy was moving toward hyperinflation and the upcoming presidential election seemed to point toward very drastic policy changes early in 1990 (probably affecting domestic public debt), no matter who won. The key question was what circumstances would prompt holders of financial assets to seek cash in order

---

ensuing month, when international markets were much closer to normal conditions and indications were clear that the central bank would not renew these dispositions. Indeed, after March 1, minimum tenure was raised to two years for borrowing and to one year for renewals. Capital inflows remained very strong until May.

FIGURE 7

OVERNIGHT INTEREST RATES AND INTERNATIONAL RESERVES,
JANUARY 1997 TO APRIL 1999

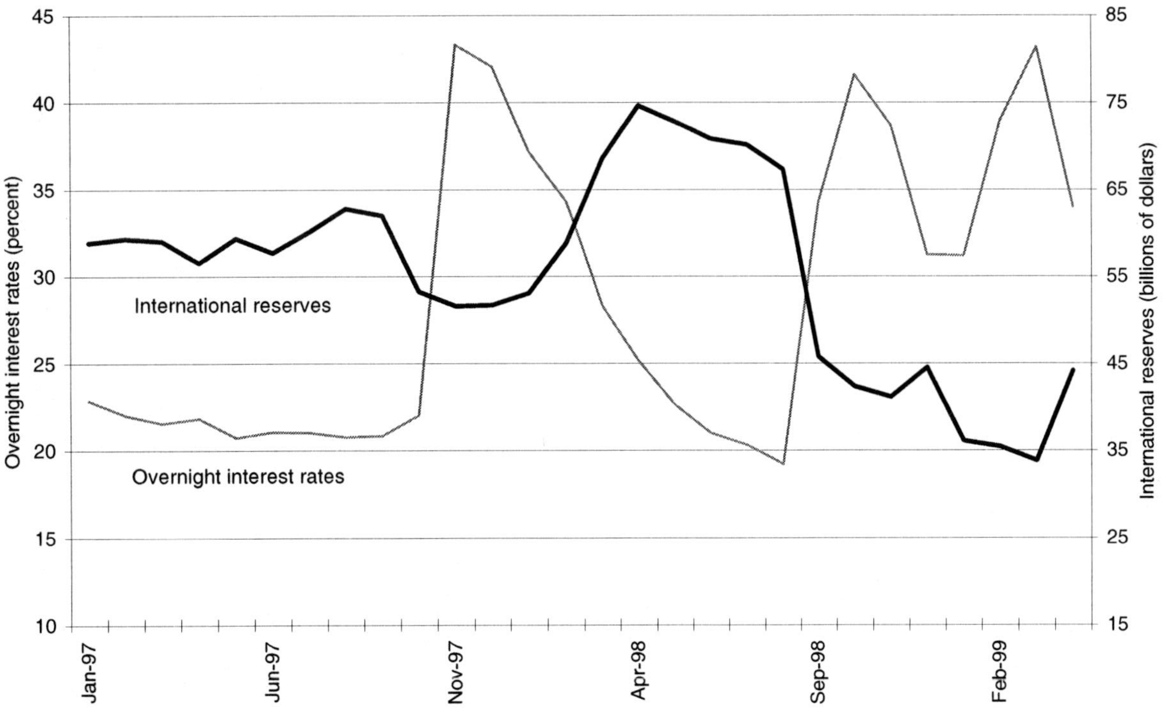

to run against international reserves so as to protect their wealth from a devaluation or from the risk of seizure by the government. Such an attack would clearly be a domestic affair and would be specific to a country having either an inconvertible currency and a deep financial market or a large publicly held domestic debt and concrete obstacles to the purchase of foreign exchange by residents.

An attack under these conditions would face two important constraints. The first would be that the convertibility regime would prevent access to international reserves by those not entitled to repatriation rights (those who could not present a registration certificate from the central bank attesting to a prior inflow of the same magnitude as the desired remittance). It is true that the amount of unused rights could be considerable, but far from true that the constraint would not be binding. The second constraint would be that there would be a natural deterrent to shifting wealth from financial assets to cash in that (1) M4 is mostly held by retail-oriented mutual funds and banks, making it somewhat immune to waves of speculative feelings, and (2) someone would have to buy these assets for cash in order to furnish the raw material for an attack. Only the central bank could do that on a large scale without provoking very substantial capital losses to the owners of that wealth.[42] If monetary accommodation were not provided, a movement like this would collapse financial-asset prices, producing huge interest-rate increases and imposing enormous *ex ante* losses that would work as a powerful deterrent to speculation. An obstacle to such accommodation could be the fragility of the banking system, which, because of restructuring efforts undertaken between 1994 and 1996, was not a factor during the Asian crisis and the turbulence following the Russian moratorium. The notion of a narrow exit is the usual argument behind the idea that foreign capital in the Brazilian stock exchange poses little risk. Even though the stock of foreign-owned equities was over US$30 billion, or about 15 percent of Brazil's total market capitalization, the São Paulo stock exchange (BOVESPA) trades, on an average active day, about US$700 million. The exit is, indeed, narrow, and investors are fully aware of that, which only suggests that portfolio investment looks, to a substantial extent, like direct investment, and not so much like "hot money." Outward flows in moments of

[42] If banks are not permitted to expand credit, only the central bank can create high-powered money. Although this seems to be the most common situation, one should understand that banks can act on the financing side of a domestic attack. This is difficult to envision for Brazil, however, given the very heavy reserve requirements imposed on the banks and the ability of the central bank to exercise suasion on them.

nervousness, even in the last quarter of 1998, were not large enough to challenge this concept (see Table 5, on p. 65).

It should be noted that when one wants to sell a domestic bond or a stock at a heavy discount, so as to attack the reserves, there is always a prior attack to be made in a domestic market, where the central bank is in a position to let prices collapse and to punish speculators. This reasoning informs the discussion on the adequacy of the stock of reserves in comparison to different measures of money stock, a theme usually raised in connection with the feasibility of, or the required reserve for, a currency board. But the issue is much more general than this. Brazil has had reserves of three to four times the money base, that is, a cover ratio much more comfortable than that of any operating currency board. It is true that M4 has been three to four times larger than international reserves, but the obstacles discussed above have served to discount very heavily the probability of attacks staged by domestic holders of government debt, especially if the domestic public debt, which has never had long maturity, has been rolled over smoothly. If this is not the case, the narrow-exit argument is weakened. The essential point here is that because domestic-debt dynamics are relevant to the strength of defenses against an attack, there is a clear connection between the exchange-rate regime and the fiscal outlook. The real importance of this connection and the perceptions about the precariousness of the domestic-debt roll-over process in Brazil have been subject to some debate.

The Brazilian authorities had little trouble rolling over domestic debt, despite the visible increase in its volume during the 1995–99 period, which included the crucial moments of the Asian crisis and the months prior to the Brazilian devaluation in January 1999 (Table 4). The Brazilian authorities have been constantly telling foreigners that the Brazilian market is essentially a domestic business, within which the participation of foreign investors is of little importance;[43] the market is, they declare, very much a captive one, where domestic retail-oriented mutual funds and banks are the dominant presence. The prices,

---

[43] The difference between domestic and foreign debt has to do with the convertibility regime. Holders of domestic debt are not authorized to remit abroad either interest or principal (this is the precise meaning of "domestic"), except when the bond was acquired through one of the specific windows designed by the central bank to attract foreign investors. One such instrument was a special class of mutual funds, designed for foreign investors, that can hold portfolios in local fixed-income instruments. The market value of these funds at their peak, in July 1998, was about US$8 billion, and the share of federal bonds in their portfolios was at least 60 percent.

the choice of maturity, and the type of indexation have always been important, because they respond to concerns about cost on the part of the Brazilian Treasury and concerns about risk on the part of the market. The growing importance of fixed-coupon paper following the stabilization represented an advance of deindexation, even though at the cost of a considerable reduction of the average maturity. By the time of the Asian crisis, the share of dollar-indexed bonds had increased from 9.3 percent in March 1997 to 15.4 percent in December, and the share of overnight interest-rate-indexed paper had reached 34.8 percent. Note that, after the Asian crisis, the share of fixed-coupon bonds rose again, reaching a peak of 55.6 percent in May 1998, at the expense of overnight indexed bonds, the share of which fell to 21.1 percent. During the second half of 1998, the market's greatest revealed concern seemed to be the interest-rate risk. This accounted for the very significant increase in overnight indexed debt (to 67 percent of the total), the minor increase in dollar-indexed bonds up to December, when it remained at 21 percent, and the near disappearance of fixed-coupon bonds.

TABLE 4

VOLUME, TYPE, AND MATURITY OF DOMESTIC FEDERAL DEBT, 1995–1999

(R$ billions)

Year	Month	Publicly Held Debt[a]	Ex- change Rate	Overnight Interest Rate	Fixed Coupons	Other[b]	Average Maturity (days)
				Type of Indexation			
1995	Dec	127.5	5.3	37.8	42.7	14.2	77
1996	Dec	189.7	9.4	18.6	61.0	11.0	116
1997	Mar	196.1	12.4	19.1	58.0	10.5	150
	Jun	201.6	9.3	19.4	60.0	11.3	190
	Sep	215.6	9.7	18.8	58.4	13.1	204
	Dec	256.7	15.4	34.8	40.9	8.9	207
1998	Mar	287.4	15.1	27.8	50.7	6.4	194
	Jun	295.8	16.5	42.7	35.1	5.7	226
	Sep	292.7	21.4	65.7	7.0	5.9	409
	Dec	323.9	21.0	69.1	3.5	6.4	n.a.
1999	Mar	365.3	25.5	68.2	1.2	5.1	n.a.

[a] Includes Treasury and central-bank bonds.

[b] Includes bonds indexed to special interest rates, such as the Taxa Referencial (TR), an average of rates in time deposits, or Taxa de Juros de Longo Prazo (TJLP), an average of coupons in dollar-indexed and dollar-denominated public debt, and bonds indexed to the price level.

SOURCE: Depec-Banco Central do Brasil.

In times of foreign-exchange distress and monetary tightening, Brazilian public displays a preference for bonds that protect aga these risks, and it is willing to pay some premium for such bonds, as compared to, say, bonds that have fixed coupons and the same duration. In minimizing the costs of rolling over domestic debt, the Treasury and the central bank constantly take advantage of market willingness to pay, in the form of foregone income or liquidity, for the hedge against interest-rate or exchange-rate fluctuations. The issuance of dollar-indexed bonds, in particular, has raised concerns that can be explained by the trauma of the Mexican tesobonos experience. Tesobonos were short-term dollar-indexed paper sold abroad for dollars in a kind of Ponzi finance game that ultimately led to a debt rescheduling (see Calvo and Mendoza, 1996). The problems involved in the episode were not related to dollar indexation as such but to the drastic shortening of Mexican external debt (or of internal debt owned by nonresidents) produced by weakening fundamentals and current-account deficits of unsustainable dimensions. This has little to do with the Brazilian experience, in which dollar-indexed bonds sold to domestic players have an average maturity of well over one year.

Derivatives: A New Battlefield

Among the most important ingredients of turbulence in Brazil's foreign-exchange market during the Asian crisis—and, indeed, until the devaluation in 1998—were foreign-exchange derivatives. The importance of derivatives for financial markets in general, and for the workings of Brazilian monetary and foreign-exchange policy in particular, can hardly be exaggerated. One expert has argued that they have become "the key development in finance in industrial countries during the last fifty years," allowing for the "commoditization" of risk in such a way and to such an extent that "derivative finance in some ways parallels the introduction of limited liability shares in the early nineteenth century" (Folkerts-Landau, 1994, pp. 574–575). The questions raised by these derivatives were new, and the workings of monetary and exchange-rate policy in Brazil had, in many ways, to be reinvented.

Foreign-exchange derivatives grew very strongly after the Real Plan and in somewhat peculiar ways. First, recall that there was no spot market within which foreign-exchange transactions could occur, unless connected to a primary transaction, that is, one between a resident and a nonresident, and subject to all authorizations and limitations. The interbank transactions were (and remain) severely limited by a mechanism that established a ceiling, at very strict numbers, to the bank's net-foreign-exchange positions, both short or long.[44] Under these restrictions, and because there was no spot market within which forwards, futures, or swaps could be settled with delivery of actual dollars, foreign-exchange derivatives were slow to develop in Brazil. Brazil was, and still is, an economy subject to what may well be called "exchange controls."

The organized derivatives exchange (Bolsa Mercantil e de Futuros [BM&F]) developed a contract through which a party agrees to pay (or receive), on a certain date, the *difference* between a certain exchange rate (implied in the contract) and the average market rate prevailing at the date of settlement. These foreign-exchange futures are, therefore, contracts settled in reals, in which the payment is the difference between spot rates on the day of closing (the last day of the month) and the rates implied on the day the contract was acquired. It is a derivative on the variation of the price of the underlying asset, *not on the spot price*, and it is important to remember that such contracts are obligations denominated in local currency, just as dollar-indexed government bonds are, and so do not represent a claim against international reserves.

The importance of foreign-exchange futures contracts grew tremendously over time. Their turnover at the BM&F expanded from US$590 million in notional value of contracts traded daily in July 1994 to US$13.3 billion traded daily in November 1997. The most visible implication of these developments was that, through arbitrage relationships, futures have gradually assumed an important role in determining the spot exchange rate. If we note that exchange-rate *policy*, or the enforcement of exchange-rate intervention bands, comprises activities through which central banks interfere in supply and demand conditions in order to affect the spot price of the foreign currency, the question very naturally is: should the authorities restrict their policy actions to the spot market or should derivatives also be subject to bands or any other intervention?

Central banks these days should hardly be surprised by this question. Currency forwards and swaps are widely used worldwide as instruments of foreign-exchange intervention and monetary policy. Futures and options are less frequently seen but are also used.[45] Experience seems to show that central banks have not been prevented from playing with

[44] The net-foreign-exchange position is the accumulated flow of purchases and sales of a given bank. The limitations are such that, all banks together may have, using possibilities to the limit, an aggregate short position of approximately US$1.5 billion.

[45] Mexico may be the most visible case of the use of currency options, puts in particular, to help enforce intervention. Many Asian countries have also been active players in this field, not always with the best results.

derivatives, especially in countries that have pegged currencies and an interest in reducing the volatility of their currencies.

The one interesting and potentially disturbing feature of these futures contracts is their leveraged impact on the spot market.[46] A speculator with R$1 million in government bonds could leverage this amount from eight to thirteen times, for instance, in short positions that communicate instantly to the spot market through arbitrage and swap operations.[47] If the pressure on futures results in a challenge to intervention points in the spot market, the involvement of international reserves required to sustain the (upper) band would be proportional to the *notional value* of (short) positions on futures. The question here is simple: should the central bank face speculators in the spot market, where its actions are limited to the stock of reserves and are at a disadvantage of ten to one, or should it shift the battle to the derivatives exchange where stakes are in reals and leveraging works both ways? Should the central bank be a player in these markets, at least in times of strain, fighting fire with fire?

The rationale for intervening in the derivatives market was largely in line with the convertibility regime: there cannot be open-ended possibilities of pressuring the spot market. This is another way of recasting the old principle that the right to remit, or the access to foreign exchange, has to be limited to previously registered inflows, or that there cannot be outflows disconnected from previous inflows.

The Banco Central do Brasil has not been inclined to impose bands on futures corresponding to those set in the spot market, but it has found it very difficult not to interfere when futures' prices, through arbitrage, have significantly challenged the corresponding intervention points in the spot market. It should be obvious that the central bank would not tolerate attacks engineered in futures markets, which would be a brand new possibility, perhaps the only one, through which residents could (almost) directly affect the exchange rate.

In October 1997, there was genuine doubt in the marketplace about whether the central bank would intervene in BM&F futures if they

[46] International evidence on whether the introduction of derivatives increases volatility in prices of the underlying asset is not conclusive. Studies point both ways, depending on the specifics of the situation (see Jochum and Kodres, 1998).

[47] The leveraging is proportional to the margin guarantees the player has to immobilize to participate in the market. These guarantees were between 2 and 5 percent of the notional values in 1997, depending on the maturity of the contract. They were raised to 7 and 12 percent after the Asian crisis and raised again at the end of 1998 to 30 percent.

were to generate significant pressure on the spot market. Indications are that there was a test on this issue and that there were signs that some foreign institutions were attempting to connect operations at the BM&F with products such as nondeliverable forwards (NDFs) sold in New York or to the Chicago Mercantile Exchange (CME), where futures in reals were also traded. But existing exchange controls made these possibilities very limited.

As it turned out, there was considerable pressure in futures in October and November 1997, until it was clearly felt that the central bank was alert to the problem. At the peak, open-interest contracts reached the equivalent of about US$40 billion in notional value, with the central bank having a significant portion of the long positions. At that time, agents who had been the usual providers of hedging in this market had been severely hit by the decline in prices of Brady bonds. The central bank had little help in the battle, but it had a decisive weapon in that it had unlimited liquidity in local currency, a crucial consideration when markets trade in predominantly nondeliverable instruments. Selling foreign-exchange futures, as they exist in Brazil, is exactly like selling dollar-indexed bonds;[48] they could thus provide a primary vehicle for short-squeezing a bear attack staged from the futures markets (as elegantly explained by Subhir Lall, 1997).[49] This was exactly what was done, and four months later, the central bank's exposure had nearly disappeared and a substantial profit had been realized. Insurance is not for free.

The obligations implied by positions taken at the BM&F should not be seen as claims against international reserves, because they would represent local-currency exposure. In discussions about the reporting of these commitments, the Brazilian position was simply to follow the consensus, to the extent that there was one, about the opening of forward books by other central banks, but with the caveat that contracts settled in domestic currency should in no circumstance be reported as an encumbrance on international reserves.

---

[48] Such a sale is technically a forward sale (purchase) of the stripped principal of a domestic government bond indexed by the exchange rate. To a substantial extent, dollar-indexed bonds of a very short maturity can be sold to those willing to carry long positions in foreign-exchange futures.

[49] The key element here is leveraging. A hedge fund in New York could buy NDFs from a bank that would enter into the opposite transaction in the BM&F, leveling its book but putting pressure on the real by leveraging. Defending the currency only in the spot market (and allowing the connection between BM&F and New York NDFs) would put the Brazilian central bank at a great disadvantage.

7   Responses to the Crisis Started by Russia

By the end of the first quarter of 1998, policymakers in Brazil had a clear sensation that their defenses against contagion from the Asian crisis had been successful. Capital was pouring in; interest rates were falling quickly; and restrictions on certain types of short-term inflows had been reinstated. The gain in international reserves between December 1997 and April 1998 was US$22.4 billion, twice the loss that had occurred between August and December 1997. Confidence was growing; the central bank's exposure in futures was insignificant; international markets were reopening; and in March 1998, the spreads on Brazilian bonds reached their lowest levels (see Figure 8). In the beginning of April, Brazil managed to issue US$1.25 billion worth of a new ten-year global bond, which, with its 375 basis-point spread, was not far from the 395 basis-point spread obtained in the thirty-year bond sold in June 1997. The issue was not smoothly executed, however, there being some slight resistance to an increase in the issue (originally set at US$1 billion), perhaps in response to the clouds already visible on the horizon. The Asian situation appeared still unsettled; Russian developments were worrisome; and there was uneasiness domestically with the fiscal numbers, which were running counter to the intentions laid out in the October 1997 package, and with the early polls for the upcoming September presidential elections, which showed a tight race between President Cardoso and his key adversary, Mr. Luiz Inácio da Silva.

A mild loss in reserves could be seen until July, when the election atmosphere began to dominate and interest rates fell more significantly. The cushion provided by reserves was seen as comfortable, even though it consisted mostly of funds of a volatile nature. The expectation was that Brazil would experience the same phenomenon that had occurred after the Mexican crisis, a slow displacement of short-term capital as higher-quality inflows resumed. Hindsight suggests that an earlier reinstatement of restrictions on short-term funds could have avoided a reserve figure of more than US$70 billion, and at the advantage of significantly smaller capital outflows and reserve losses in September, when the Russian crisis hit Brazil.

The Russian moratorium introduced a financial turbulence that was much more disturbing than the Asian crisis, at least with regard to Brazil. It launched a worldwide reassessment of investment in emerging markets by all classes of international investors and financial institutions. This had a deep impact on Brazil in view of Brazil's 30 to 45 percent share in emerging-market portfolios and of the specific hedging strategies used by investors directly enduring losses in Russia. The results of

FIGURE 8

SPREADS ON THE J.P. MORGAN EMERGING MARKET BOND INDEX (EMBI)

these developments on the spreads of Brazilian securities leave no doubt about the seriousness of this crisis relative to the previous one (see Figure 8).

These effects, as well as the extent of the contagion of the Russian decision to other regions through the Brady-bond markets, were by no means anticipated. The position of the G–7 on the Russian moratorium seemed to conform to the statements heard from the G–22 during the spring 1998 IMF meeting on the issue of sharing the burden of future rescue packages with the private sector. The successive IMF programs undertaken with Asian countries raised the usual criticism about program design, but the critics appeared to hit an especially sensitive cord on the issue of moral hazard. Mixed incentives might be produced in other countries undertaking reforms if it was thought that a bailout would always be available in case of need. Russia, in particular, represented a clear challenge in this respect. Market participants and rating agencies were said to "price in" the bailout in light of specific political or national-security considerations. A former U.K. prime minister, also a member of a famous hedge-fund board, was quoted as saying that if the Americans had spent trillions of dollars to fight Russia, they would not hesitate to spare a few billion to settle the economic issue definitively and peacefully.

By all indications, the Russian decision was assisted by the IMF staff, it being even argued that the "haircut" imposed on Russian debt was tailored to fit the fiscal projections of the IMF's program. Whether true or not, this is the version that counts for the markets. It may be unfair to blame the IMF for this event, too, but the fact is that the official sector vastly underestimated both the impact of this decision on market perceptions of risk in emerging markets and the capacity of the owners of Russian securities to shift the burdens of the moratorium elsewhere. The contagion was thus much more extensive than that seen during the Asian crisis. Burden sharing had become burden shifting, and countries far away from Russia, geographically and economically, were obliged to pay an unduly high price for problems that were not theirs. The IMF may have created the moral obligation to help innocent bystanders, if need be, but could Brazil be included among these innocent injured parties?

Aggravating Circumstances

The agent for spreading the contagion of the Russian crisis into Brazil was the market for Brady bonds. The considerable deleveraging in this market in response to the losses incurred through the Asian crisis had reduced the direct repercussions of the collapse of Russian bonds on Brazilian banks and on mutual funds of Brazilian origin. But the pressure now was much stronger. In the presence of the ongoing general reassessment of risk, which became more negative in September with the failure of the Long Term Capital Management (LTCM) hedge fund, Brazilian securities would suffer an extraordinary pressure to sell and to sell quickly. In addition, hedging strategies for long positions in Russian instruments would very commonly be constructed with a short position against the J.P. Morgan Emerging Market Bond Index (EMBI), a composite of the main Brady bonds in the market, or against the Brazilian C bond, which although it represented only 4 percent of the EMBI, was, by far, the most traded emerging-market instrument at the time. More specifically, short-selling the C bond and, to a lesser extent, the Interest Due Unpaid (IDU) bond,[50] became common, and there seemed to be no question that the way it was done was meant to drive the price downward, which would reduce losses in Russia.

It is notable that the U.S. securities law includes restrictions about the repeated use of short-selling by a broker. Rule 10a-1, known as the "Tick Rule," states that a second short sale of a given security cannot be made at a price lower than the exchange reference price, the tick. The rule would be difficult to implement in the context of Brady bonds, for which trading occurs all over the planet with no reference price being fixed in any exchange or jurisdiction. Its mention in this context, however, points to a clear regulatory asymmetry between domestic (U.S.) and offshore markets that was detrimental to market integrity and that amplified the contagion of the Russian default to other emerging economies.[51]

It was also the case that the aggregate amounts short-sold in C bonds appeared to be out of proportion to amounts available in the market place. Difficulties in delivery could be seen everywhere, producing the highly unusual phenomenon of negative interest rates for repurchase operations with C bonds and also with IDU bonds, a condition that is said to mean that the security is rich, that is, that it will rise shortly.[52]

[50] The IDU bond was issued by Brazil, shortly before the agreement with the creditors, along lines similar to the Brady Plan. It is one of the most traded emerging-market debt instruments.

[51] There are also rules regarding margins on short sales—such as Regulation T of the U.S. Federal Reserve Board—that do not generally apply to offshore trading.

[52] A typical repurchase (repo) operation involves the sale (purchase) of the bond with a repurchase (sale) agreement at a given price. It is like lending (borrowing) the security, or borrowing (lending) money. When the repurchase rate is negative, it means that

Indeed, if the delivery were forced by the buyers, short sellers could not sustain their positions for very long. Borrowing securities from Euroclear could, in this case, postpone the delivery, but not by much. For securities traded offshore, the only procedure available to force delivery—and then to drive short-sellers to buy the bonds on spot to cover their positions—would be the buy-in provisions under the International Securities Market Association (ISMA) rules and recommendations (Rule 451 of Section 450), to which trading houses subscribe on a voluntary basis. The procedure is cumbersome but could work if pursued to the end. Yet, even though there were substantial sales of C bonds, technically on default, very few buy-in procedures were taken to advanced stages. The common complaint of Brazilian investment banks, which were usually on the long side of the deal, was that the procedure almost invariably produced threats and retaliations on the part of the market makers, which happened to be large international banks that no one wanted to confront. Again, a regulatory asymmetry favoring the large market maker over the smaller player challenging a short sale was detrimental to market integrity.

These examples are meant only to highlight the mechanics of contagion and to show how the Brady-bond markets have become important in this connection.[53] It is also true that almost all the borrowing done by emerging markets, particularly in Latin America, occurs through the issuance of bonds, the pricing of which is formed in direct connection with secondary markets. If these markets are subject to manipulation and unfair practices that distort pricing, regulation is certainly in order.[54] Yet, regulators in the G–7 have shown hesitation and skepticism on the issue, because, as they rightly argue, restrictions will make business migrate offshore. Emphasis has been placed on the interface between banks and other entities such as nonbank players and participants based offshore. This may not be enough to prevent banks from assuming unduly large risks, and it has certainly not been enough to ensure market integrity in the field of Brady bonds.

---

someone needs the security so badly that he borrows it, that is, he lends money against the security at a negative rate.

[53] Another interesting example along these lines is the one provided by Hong Kong, where short-selling in the stock exchange by players offshore was used as an instrument to attack the currency. The Hong Kong Monetary Authority (HKMA) subsequently changed regulations governing short sales, introducing strict rules obliging delivery.

[54] A pledge to regulate such transactions is usually made in connection with the actions of hedge funds, for which it is widely recognized that regulation on the grounds of market integrity makes sense (see Eichengreen et al., 1998).

Once again, primary issues were completely paralyzed. Brady-bond and corporate-bond spreads were comparable to what was seen in the worst moments of the Mexican crisis, or to the levels seen when the original Brady deals were struck. There were substantial outflows from Brazil in order to buy back not only Brady bonds and global bonds, but also corporate bonds. It would not be difficult to argue that these outflows were healthy and were driven by an arbitrage opportunity that, once enjoyed, would correct the mispricing of Brady bonds and, eventually, revive primary issues. It was annoying, however, that in the presence of unrestricted short-selling and the difficulties of starting buy-in procedures, the arbitrage outflows from Brazil were, although large, not sufficient to change prices, let alone bring them back to a point at which primary issues would be viable again. This highlights the fact that for capital-account convertibility to be advantageous to countries like Brazil, some regulatory framework should be put in place.

The composition of the very impressive reserve losses experienced by Brazil in the last five months of 1998 points to the nature of the pressures affecting the country (see Table 5). Note that the current-account deficit reported in the table includes leads and lags in foreign trade and is, thus, not the same current-account concept normally reported in balance-of-payments statistics. Leads and lags are normally capital inflows, but from August through December 1998, the accumulated loss of trade lines, resulting in more payments in cash for imports as proportion of imports cleared and fewer advances on exports to be shipped as proportion of exports shipped, could be estimated at about US$10 billion. The current-account deficit measured by the usual criteria was US$18.6 billion. Although this figure is larger than the US$14.1 billion obtained by the criteria used in Table 5, it should be larger still.

The loss of short-term capital parked in instruments designed for "hot money," the very same instruments that the central bank was slow to restrict in the first quarter of 1998 (fixed-income funds and Resolution 63 [agriculture] in Table 5) approached US$11 billion. Some tax measures to encourage their permanence were attempted, but with little success. The only good news was that these outflows were sharply reduced when the previously formed stock of registered inflows was being exhausted by the end of the year. The outflows from the floating-rate market, which reached US$16.6 billion in the period covered by Table 5, should be very carefully interpreted. Because there are a lot of service imports flowing only through this channel, an outflow of US$1 billion to US$1.5 billion a month is considered normal. For the

TABLE 5

BALANCE OF PAYMENTS AND RESERVE LOSSES, AUGUST TO DECEMBER 1998

(*US$ millions*)

	Aug	Sep	Oct	Nov	Dec	Total
"Current account"[a]	−1,582	−4,699	−3,435	−1,606	−2,822	−14,144
Trade balance[a]	−26	−781	−1,042	96	2	−1,751
Services	−1,556	−3,918	−2,393	−1,702	−2,824	−12,393
Interest	−541	−1,210	−1,265	−866	−1,372	−5,254
Dividends	−359	−1,858	−476	−424	−843	−3,960
Other	−656	−850	−652	−412	−609	−3,179
Short-term capital	−8,083	−15,832	−4,392	−464	−3,048	−31,819
Fixed-income funds	−2,383	−3,652	−436	−23	−15	−6,509
Resolution 63 (agriculture)	−1,792	−1,375	−614	−272	−375	−4,428
Brady-bond funds (Fiex)	−489	−842	43	712	75	−501
Portfolio (annexes I to V)	−1,539	−1,688	−63	348	−845	−3,787
Floating-rate market	−1,880	−8,275	−3,322	−1,229	−1,888	−16,594
Long-term capital	5,276	−331	5,044	116	655	10,760
FDI	4,567	2,356	3,747	1,822	1,521	14,013
Loans	4,190	1,077	5,733	891	2,784	14,675
Amortizations	−3,133	−3,125	−3,508	−2,523	−3,548	−15,837
Resolution 63 (other)	−348	−639	−928	−74	−102	−2,091
Other	1,511	−660	−641	758	−798	170
Operations with the IMF	—	—	—	—	9,324	9,324
Change in int'l reserves	−2,878	−21,522	−3,424	−1,196	3,311	−25,709
Level of int'l reserves	67,333	45,111	42,385	41,501	35,177[b]	—

[a] The "current account" includes the trade balance and services. The trade balance is reported according to a "payments concept," that is, it includes leads and lags in trade, as well as amortization, for exports and imports, if the lending (borrowing) is inferior to one year. For this reason, the "current account" reported does not correspond to that normally appearing in the balance-of-payments statistics.

[b] Excluding the drawings from the IMF and BIS facilities.

SOURCE: Banco Central do Brasil.

amounts exceeding these numbers, central-bank reports suggested three motivations: (1) hot-money outflows, that is, unregistered fixed-income investments made by nonresidents into Brazil through the so-called CC5 accounts;[55] (2) arbitrage operations undertaken by residents with Brady bonds, and the repurchase by companies of their own bonds

[55] The CC5 accounts are special accounts that are in local currency but are freely convertible to hard currency. They were created by the Banco Central do Brasil in 1969 through Carta Circular 5 (thus, the CC5 denomination) for nonresidents temporarily in Brazil. Their scope was subsequently broadened.

at enormous discounts; and (3) capital-flight movements prompted by the loss of confidence by residents in domestic policies. In view of the heavy concentration of outflows in September, one may assume that the first two motives were dominant, but this is hard to ascertain.

Note that the outflows from equity-portfolio investment were small considering the size of positions held by nonresidents and the outflows from fixed-income investments. This again confirms the observation made above that the narrow exit door deterred large outflows from this source. The US$3.7 billion in outflows are less than 10 percent of the total market capitalization and less than 25 percent of all portfolios held by foreigners. During these five months, the market capitalization of the BOVESPA index fell from US$234 billion in July to US$161 billion in December, a loss about twenty times larger than the outflow! The FDI inflows only seemed strong; the inflows observed could be explained by the Telebrás privatization, partly settled in August, and by a couple of large acquisitions in the banking sector in September and October. Part of the revenues associated with the Telebrás sale coming due in 2000 could be anticipated as a large loan in October. Other than that, the activity in long-term borrowing was very modest, not to say altogether nil.

The magnitude of these outflows combined with pessimism about the repercussions of the credit tightening caused by reactions to the Russian moratorium and the LTCM failure composed a gloomy picture. The U.S. Federal Reserve's reductions in interest rates helped somewhat, but the Brazilian situation could not be improved much in view of one crucial aggravating circumstance: the present position called for a response similar to the one engineered for the Asian crisis. On September 10, two weeks before the presidential election, the central bank's monetary-policy committee (COPOM) held an extraordinary meeting at which it raised interest rates to 40 percent in an attempt to elicit just such a response. The move elicited some political fatigue, as it appeared that belts would be tightened yet again, but, most important, it showed that a response similar to that of 1997 was no longer available, because the failure of the earlier promised fiscal effort to deliver had produced a serious credibility gap. An effort of 2 percent of GDP had been promised when the PSBR was already at 6 percent. A year later, in September 1998, the PSBR was at 8.3 percent and climbing. It would appear that only after the election would the issue be revisited, and indications that the next term would be development oriented were by no means encouraging. Markets had believed the promise in 1997 and had reacted accordingly. Now, they were completely unwilling to forgive what was seen as a serious breach of confidence. Brazil was faced with a problem that it could not solve on its own. If policymakers could not deliver fiscal discipline in 1997, how could they deliver it now?

The Agreement with the IMF

There were at least two novel features in the Brazilian initiative to seek IMF assistance late in September. First, in contrast to all past occasions, both sides shared the same view this time about what should be done: the critical issue was enforceability of fiscal discipline. The Brazilian authorities were ready to propose an effort that would be seen as large enough to negate the bad impression left by the failure of the October 1997 fiscal package, but they wanted to present the program as theirs, not as a condition imposed by the IMF. The IMF did not object. The second feature was that the Brazilians were coming to the IMF *before* any negative event or crisis, that is, before a devaluation or a moratorium, and with the very clear and firm intention of preventing either outcome. This situation was uncommon and called for new strategies.

Brazil was seen as a key piece in the game of contagion chess, and in early October 1998, at the annual meeting of the IMF and World Bank in Washington, D.C., the Brazilian authorities forcibly made the point that they wanted a preventive program to defend the currency, that it should have a fiscal emphasis, and that it should include money that would be used only in case of need. Both the IMF and the official sector showed great sympathy with the concept of prevention, although with understandable nuances. President Clinton himself mentioned several times the intention of creating a "new precautionary facility" to insulate countries with good records in market-oriented reforms against shocks originating in other parts of the world. The president repeated these remarks when he personally addressed the G–22 countries in Washington, and rumors were that a "Contingent Reserve Facility" would be created at the IMF, to be used first by Brazil. Contingent Credit Lines (CCLs) were, indeed, created at the IMF, but later, in April 1999. By all indications, Brazil was to be a test of this new, preventive, concept.

The idea of a precautionary facility presented a number of implementation problems. First, a program conducted before a crisis should place much more emphasis on structural benchmarks and reforms facilitating fiscal balance, private savings, and systemic efficiency and growth than on the financial-programming targets typical of IMF conditionality based on rigorous compliance with targets for PSBRs, net domestic assets (NDAs), and net international reserves (NIRs). Brazil's program tried to have both, and there was some tension about which portion of the program was really the critical one.

Second, the question of how much money was needed was complicated by the fact that it was not the usual matter of estimating the financing needs for the program's duration. Stretching the numbers for such needs, using slightly pessimistic assumptions, one could arrive at a figure of US$20 billion for 1999. By midyear, it appeared that US$15 billion would be sufficient, even with the turbulence during the first semester. Aside from the program money, Brazil had US$35 billion in reserves, even after the great cleanup during the five months from August to December (Table 5). Because the key issue for a preventive program was to restore confidence, choosing the size of the package was clearly a subjective exercise directed at impressing markets. If the market estimate was US$30 billion, then the amount allocated should be more. In the end, the package was fixed at US$41.5 billion, with a disbursement schedule described as heavily front-loaded: two-thirds of the money could be used in the first year. There was also some difficulty in saying that the program's success would be measured by its *not using* the money. Although it would be wonderful if such an announcement could, alone, rebuild confidence, it was unlikely to do so, given the depth of the crisis and the additional fact that some of the official money promised to the Koreans, at the time of their rescue package in 1997, had not materialized. Rather, the money *should* be used, as an indication that the program was real; its use should not be read as the program's failure. The authorities walked a narrow line in defining this discourse and the amounts to draw.

Third, the official sector's political demands about how to involve the private banks in the scheme became very difficult to satisfy. For a preventive program, the old steering-committee routine typical of rescheduling exercises, was anathema. In fact, every hostile movement would most likely scare the banks away from the program and reduce its chances of success. Because the point was to recover confidence, the Brazilians insisted that the strategy with regard to private-sector banks and investors should be the "open road show," the instrument usually deployed by a borrower to expose its prospects and invite subscriptions on the basis of unconstrained market judgment. In this case, the strategy was even more market friendly, because there was no borrowing to be done, only the interruption of exposure-reduction measures, especially in the field of trade and interbank lines. Bond sales, possibly aiming at re-funding the program, could be concluded later, as markets returned to normalcy. Eventually, however, the Brazilian authorities had to compromise and combine open presentations with smaller meetings attended by central bankers and IMF officials. In Europe, this seemed more natural than in the United States. It was, however, difficult to reconcile the demands for tough talk and strict monitoring of the banks with the voluntary character that participation in a preventive program should have had.

The program was essentially ready by mid-October. President Cardoso was reelected in the first round of voting, and by November, the markets were much more relaxed and outflows had sharply decelerated. As seen in Table 5, the reserve loss in November was a little more than US$1 billion, and Brazil was about to disburse the first tranche of the loan, which should have been in excess of US$9 billion. Again, there had been some pressure on futures markets: the value of open-interest contracts reached the notional equivalent of US$36 billion in October, again with the central bank having a significant stake on the long side. On December 1, however, when pressures had receded, the central bank withdrew altogether from this market. On December 2, the IMF's board approved the Brazilian program, there being no indication of significant additional reductions in trade lines from foreign banks in the days prior to its decision, as had been feared by the official sector.

The necessity of submitting the agreement to the Senate's approval postponed the drawings to December 15 and 18, when the outlook had taken a substantial turn for the worse.[56] The bad news had started on December 9, when the government unexpectedly lost an important vote on a bill related to social security contributions; it continued into January, with Minas Gerais state governor Itamar Franco, former president of Brazil, declaring a moratorium on his state's obligations to the federal government. Other opposition governors suggested they might follow suit, and, all of a sudden, markets became extremely nervous. This demonstrated how sensitive the whole arrangement was to the government's capacity to deliver its fiscal promises or to any deviation from the program's fiscal targets.

[56] The program was structured in two parallel parts: (1) a Standby Arrangement (SBA) combined with the Supplementary Reserve Facility (SRF) based at the IMF, and (2) a facility based at the Bank for International Settlements (BIS), comprising funds from twenty countries to be drawn in conditions identical to the SRF drawings. Every drawing by Brazil would consist of two parallel drawings, the BIS portion usually becoming available a few days later than the IMF portion.

By the end of the year, these events also confirmed that, in view of the size of the package and the concerns displayed, the return of confidence would be much more gradual than had originally been imagined by the IMF and the official sector. The critical element would be Brazil's initiative with respect to its own problems, which was an ongoing issue not likely to be settled quickly. The bad news in December was simply a political test of the government's resolve, similar to prior tests and to others to come. Even though the quantitative implications of both the lost vote and Itamar Franco's initiative were small, the government's reaction was decisive to the program's credibility. The central bank had made it clear that such conditions could very well result in a monetary tightening or, at the very least, some delay in the widely demanded interest-rate reduction.

The Regime Change and Its Consequences

As was later revealed, the president had been considering changes in economic policy since September. Indications at that time were ambiguous. On the one hand, there were signs that the president wanted his second term to be more development oriented. "He who finished inflation will also do away with unemployment," was a popular campaign motto. This development rhetoric had very specific and worrisome implications for fiscal policy and for the mix of interest rates and exchange rates. The president never failed, however, to support existing policies when the need arose. In his crucial speech at the Itamaraty palace on September 22, 1999, he acknowledged for the first time during the campaign the seriousness of the crisis, and he proposed a major mobilization for the balancing of the budget as a final solution to the country's vulnerability. Except for the idea that a ministry of production would be created, nothing in the speech deviated from the basic lines of existing policy.

Meanwhile, the first numbers for the targeted variables, most notably the PSBRs, seemed to have been easily met for December and, most likely, for January, too.[57] The NDA target, although missed for December had a very good chance of being met in January. In such circumstances, who would be willing to discuss the instability of money demand in the month of December? A waiver was actually ready to be submitted entitling the Brazilians, if they so desired, to accelerate the drawing of the second tranche to the beginning of February.

[57] In fact, the IMF's insistence in reckoning the nominal PSBR instead of the primary surplus (PSBR minus nominal interest payments) made the target very sensitive to the nominal interest rate.

The political atmosphere, however, was indeed clouded. Cardoso was starting a new term obliged to play, as he had for the past year and a half, a tough defense. It was frustrating that after four years of fighting for the consolidation of stabilization and the initiation of reforms, no benefits in terms of economic growth could yet be reaped. It was true that exogenous events had played a crucial part in that stasis; two financial crises of planetary dimensions, from which Brazil could not possibly hide, had induced a change in plans. In the political world, however, this was just another excuse: the promises for rapid growth, better income distribution, and more attention to social problems as Brazil advanced with the stabilization and reform program could not be kept. Nobody would bother to remember that the fallout from the Asian and the Russian crises might have been much worse in the absence of the Real Plan. The opposition, and very substantial segments of the São Paulo business community, strongly argued that the Real Plan only made Brazil more vulnerable to external shocks. Devaluation, protectionism, subsidies, and lower interest rates were preached everywhere, and the president was pressed to offer alternatives. Opinions were divided within the government. Some thought the reelection reflected Brazilians' desire for continuity; others thought the campaign promises for development and change were crucial.

All serious discussions of alternatives considered the exchange-rate regime and ways to accomplish a permanent reduction in interest rates soon after the acute moments of the crisis had passed. It was duly recognized that the exchange-rate regime had been very successful in bringing Brazil beyond hyperinflation, deindexation, trade liberalization, and the consolidation of stabilization and introduction of reforms. But the two crises provoked several questions, some new, some very old, that would beg for new or renewed definitions. Apart from the broad issue of the optimal choice of exchange-rate regime, several important features of the Brazilian crawling-band experience should be remarked.

Crucial to the decisions made at the end of 1998 was a precise understanding of the monetary-policy implications of an exchange-rate regime involving a crawl, be it a band or a peg. In order not to provoke capital outflows in such a regime, the domestic interest rate, deducting the crawl, should provide a rate of return as least as high as the one available from a dollar-denominated Brazilian security abroad.[58] Note that if the crawl were exactly equal to inflation—as

[58] The cleanest arbitrage relationship was the one between a domestic Treasury security having the overnight interest rate as remuneration and a Brazilian Brady bond to be held on a repurchase basis for the same maturity.

71

was typical of past crawling pegs, which were invented to prevent real appreciation produced by inflation—the real interest rate would be more or less identical to the external interest rate. If, however, the crawl were to run faster than inflation, there would be (1) a gradual *real* devaluation, and (2) a real interest rate higher than would otherwise be the case. This means that, in order to prevent capital flight, a crawl that is meant to devalue the real exchange rate has to be implemented at the cost of additions to the real interest rate, and *the higher the real interest rate, the faster will be the desired real devaluation.* In the Brazilian case, the argument was made using numbers along the following lines: taking the C bond as the foreign security used in arbitrage, the floor to the domestic interest rate would be equal to the yield on the C bond at, say, 10 or 11 percent (that is, spreads over U.S. Treasury rates of 500 or 600 basis points), plus the devaluation implied in the existing crawl (7.5 percent), plus other terms standing for taxation, transfer risk, and such things. The floor was taken to be 19 or 20 percent, being lower at friendly market times, when the yields for the C bond fell by more than 400 basis points. Under inflation rates of, say, 10 percent, the real interest rate would be thoroughly "international," or similar to the yield on the C bond. If inflation were zero, as it was in 1998, an interest-rate floor of 19 or 20 percent would be an entirely different proposition. Besides, after the Russian moratorium, the yields on the C bond climbed to 1,800 basis points, which would put the floor for domestic interest rates above 35 percent a year, levels that, under zero inflation, would be incredibly high. This was a crisis situation, however, and even in the absence of the crawl, the real interest rates required to prevent capital outflows, considering the atypical state and the extremely depressed prices of the C bond, would have to be extraordinarily high. Yet, real rates this high could not fail to bring comparisons with Russia and to elicit concerns about the fiscal sustainability of such a stance.

Even if we abstract from the crisis situation, however, it is still true that a crawling-band regime intended to produce some impact on the real exchange rate would require a real interest rate of some size. If a real-exchange-rate devaluation were no longer desired, the crawl could be suspended, the band could be enforced without a drift, and nothing would prevent the domestic interest rate from approaching the yields on the C bond except, of course, fiscal policy. If, however, some additional real-exchange-rate depreciation were needed, the question would arise of the exact distance to be covered by the crawl. This was, again, a judgment about the alleged overvaluation or about where the ideal, or the equilibrium, real exchange rate should be. This was the issue that mobilized discussions with the IMF and the official sector during the design of the Brazilian program. The continuation of existing policies would deliver an approximately 7.5 percent real devaluation in 1999, and probably another round in 2000, on top of about 8 percent accomplished in 1998. Because interest rates would be high, at least for a few months, in light of the existing yields on the C bond, it would be reasonable to expect that the subject of the floor in interest rates entered discussions again only in the second semester. Was the additional 7.5 percent enough, or was it too little at the cost of too high interest rates for too long?

This decision implied, of course, a discussion of alternatives. One that was very popular was the idea of a faster crawl, a suggestion made loudly by economists from opposition parties but also, surprisingly, by some members of the IMF staff. The obvious problem with a faster crawl was that it would put the floor for interest rates at even higher levels. Another alternative, floating the currency, was too risky to begin right in the middle of the turbulence. Floating could lead to an uncontrolled Asian-style megadevaluation, the consequences of which for inflation and for neighboring countries would be totally unpredictable. The risk of destroying the stabilization effort was concrete, and very few, if any, observers proposed floating, except for the future, after things had calmed down. Intermediate alternatives were considered, but the majority view was that innovation was difficult at such a critical moment and especially inconvenient after considerable time, effort, and money had been devoted to an agreement to defend existing policies.

The president, however, was convinced that a change should be attempted, and this stance provoked the resignation of the central-bank governor, who opposed any policy change at that point. The president's decision was not a clear-cut option for a float; he had first supported the introduction of a complicated arrangement called an "endogenous diagonal band." This band had collapsed within forty-eight hours, however, and, as every other remaining sign of credibility was lost, the float was forced. Dr. Francisco Lopes, the newly appointed governor of the central bank, resigned even before his formal inauguration, after two weeks of an uncontrolled devaluation. Before Dr. Arminio Fraga was appointed governor and took over on March 8, the real had reached R$2.16, an astounding 77 percent devaluation with respect to the R$1.22 in place when the innovation was attempted.

No indication of these changes was ever mentioned to the IMF or to the official sector before they were implemented, and it is no wonder that there was considerable difficulty in subsequently reconstructing the agreement with the IMF. What was to have been avoided at all costs was then peacefully surrendered, and defenses were immediately and strongly reinforced. The assumption of a preventive agreement was thoroughly destroyed, and the program with the IMF was downgraded to an ordinary crisis-resolution program, having lost all the novel features initially included. It would appear that the failure of this first attempt at a preventive effort was stymied, quite surprisingly, by the program beneficiary's own free will. When the CCLs were created in April 1999, IMF managing director, Michel Camdessus, was asked whether Brazil would have been eligible for the credit lines had they been available in December 1998; he was quoted as saying, "It would have been the mistake of the year."

The new program differed significantly from the first attempt. The relevant PSBR target was now the primary surplus, rather than the nominal PSBR, which had been driven to unthinkable numbers by the devaluation (the direct fiscal impact of which was estimated at 11 percent of GDP). Compliance with the financial-program target was made much stricter; the central bank's freedom to intervene in foreign-exchange markets and futures was severely curtailed; and the consultation clauses regarding monetary policy were strengthened. The estimates for GDP growth for 1999 were fixed at –3.5 percent, in contrast to the –1 percent set in the first memorandum, and inflation estimates were raised to 17 percent (for the IGP-DI). Given the projected exchange rate for the end of the year of R$1.70, it could be assumed that a round 20 percent real devaluation was sought.

The effect on inflation was, at first, frightening and prompted a number of alarming forecasts. February inflation measured by the IGP-FGV was 4.44 percent (with WPI inflation at almost 7 percent), and inflation might continue to rise, depending on the way in which the government would handle the decisions, due May 1, about the readjustment of the minimum wage, the readjustment of prices of utilities tied to dollar clauses, and the transmission of WPI inflation into the CPI. Yet, much to the surprise of most observers, the inflationary impact receded; March and April inflation rates measured by the IGP-FGV were 1.98 percent and 0.03 percent, respectively, with an unexpectedly modest 7.75 percent accumulated rate for the year to April. A deflation was expected for May. The interest rate had been raised to 45 percent before the end of January, and the brutal recession in the making, in addition to the fact that the exchange rate rapidly returned to levels of about R$1.65, prevented further inflationary repercussions from the

74

devaluation. It was with a not inconsiderable sense of relief that Brazilians learned that the indexation virus had been effectively destroyed. The previous five years of deindexation, deregulation, and market-oriented reforms had yielded a very clear payoff.

The most important surprise in the devaluation episode was the very limited impact it had on inflation. It seemed that the central bank had armed itself for a fierce battle in this field, loudly announcing the implementation of inflation targets just when inflation forecasts suggested that the IMF's assumption of 17 percent was unrealistically low. But the unexpectedly mild numbers on inflation meant that interest rates could be lowered much more quickly than expected, and the recession appeared likely to be much softer than had been anticipated in the IMF memorandum. Although the devaluation was not the inflation-recession catastrophe most people expected, its fiscal impacts were devastating and the trade-balance response was sluggish at best. It is true that commodity prices, except for oil, were at their lowest levels in twenty-five years and that trade lines available for exporters were severely depleted. Moreover, all the uncertainties about what the exchange-rate regime would be, and, especially, the still-uncertain commitment to a given medium-term exchange-rate level, made it difficult for exporters and importers to make decisions.

Meanwhile, crisis recovery seemed well under way. Capital outflows stopped; the more speculative inflows slowed; Brady-bond prices started to recover; primary issues once again became viable; some of the safer credits resumed raising money through very short-term channels; foreign banks again extended lines of credit; and local affiliates of multinational companies started to borrow from parent companies. In April, the government went to the market, this time raising US$3 billion, two-thirds of it in cash and the remaining in exchange for IDU and EI bonds.[59] The term was for five years and the spread of 650 basis points was an eloquent demonstration of a new pricing reality.

The atmosphere was starting to improve. Privatizations resumed with the sale of Comgás (the gas company of the state of São Paulo) for approximately US$1 billion, and privatization revenues of approximately US$20 billion were estimated for the reminder of 1999. Reserve losses were arrested after additional blows early in the year (see Table 6). Excluding the US$19.2 disbursed from the IMF, reserves fell to US$25.1

[59] Like the IDU bond, the Eligible Interest (EI) bond was issued before Brazil entered the Brady Plan. Both the IDUs and EIs rescheduled interest past due, and both had coupons related to the London interbank offer rate (LIBOR).

TABLE 6

BALANCE OF PAYMENTS AND RESERVE LOSSES, JANUARY TO APRIL 1999

(US$ million)

"Current account"[a]	−6,408
Trade balance[a]	2,298
Services	−8,706
Short-term capital	−5,171
Fixed-income funds	1,905
Resolution 63 (agriculture)	−1,134
Brady-bond funds (Fiex)	n.a.
Portfolio (annexes I to V)	714
Floating-rate market	−3,728
Other	−2,928
Long-term capital	499
FDI	9,150
Loans	12,845
Amortizations	−21,505
Other	1,194
Operations with the IMF	9,845
Change in international reserves	−41
Int'l reserves including drawings from the IMF and BIS	44,315
Int'l reserves excluding drawings from the IMF and BIS	25,146

[a] The "current account" includes the trade balance and services. The trade balance is reported according to a "payments concept," that is, it includes leads and lags in trade, as well as amortization, for exports and imports, if the lending (borrowing) is inferior to one year. For this reason, the "current account" reported does not correspond to that normally appearing in the balance-of-payments statistics.

SOURCE: Banco Central do Brasil.

billion. Given these conditions, the exchange rate appreciated rapidly to R$1.63, at the lowest point in May, and some observers showed concern that Brazil might return to the August 1994 dilemma, in which to continue with an unconstrained floating-exchange-rate regime could mean to accept an undesirable appreciation. In fact, if markets were to keep improving, the continuation of the float might bring the real exchange rate to levels very close to those that might have been reached had the old crawling bands been maintained. The situation seemed to require the authorities to choose between allowing the erosion of the real-exchange-rate gains of the devaluation or considering the introduction of some form of systematic intervention. Neither decision could be taken lightly.

The problem was postponed, however, by the increasing concerns about the future of Argentina's currency board, which depressed market outlook and stopped the appreciation trend. The real started to depreciate, climbing back to levels of about R$2, while the central bank continued to reduce interest rates. In October, when interest rates reached precrisis levels (19 percent), it appeared that the recession had been avoided but that the risks of an overheated economy and of an inflationary burst were very much present. At this point, although CPI inflation was running safely within targets (about 8 percent), WPI inflation was at 30 percent. This divergent behavior in the indices had been seen before. This time, the preferred interpretation was that it presaged danger; the usual train of events would be for the WPI inflation to anticipate the CPI inflation. The macroeconomic atmosphere was deteriorating rapidly in the third quarter of 2000, when the central bank finally started to move after a frustrated attempt to replace finance minister Pedro Malan in October. Interest rates were kept at 19 percent, and the exchange rate was forced to appreciate slowly. The inflationary threat was averted, and by the end of the year, the issue of reforms again edged toward the forefront of the political agenda. A virtuous cycle was reinstated, with confidence increasing as the real grew stronger and the WPI inflation started to converge to the CPI inflation level. As noted in Figure 2, real exchange rates are not now very far from the levels where they would have been had the old crawl been continued. The exchange-rate regime, moreover, has been subject to so much intervention that the "floating" rhetoric has been carefully avoided by the authorities. It appears that a new compromise between rigidity and flexibility is in the making.

8 Conclusions

Two questions have been saved for this conclusion. First, what general lessons may be drawn from the choices of exchange-rate policies made in Brazil under differing circumstances and in response to complex and overlapping agendas of stabilization and reform. Second, what progress has been accomplished by the Real Plan, after six years, with respect to structural reform and development prospects. The choice of exchange-rate policies was, after all, always conditioned by the broader prospects of development and change.

Is There Anything between the Extremes?

After all these years, the exchange-rate regime in Brazil has undergone many changes. Brazil went through a brief experience with a float, then adopted an informal, and later a formal European-style, target-zone system. This was then given a drift and became a crawling-bands system, which was maintained for a few years with a view toward greater flexibility. Later, after the second major international crisis in approximately one year, Brazil returned to a float. After an initial overshooting, the central bank regained control of the market and has actively avoided spurious volatility. The system may or may not return to a target zone, but is not difficult to see conditions under which this could happen.

It is tempting to see a cycle in this trajectory and to conclude that the optimal choice of exchange-rate regime is, after all, heavily dependent on domestic circumstances, traditions, and institutional realities, as well as on the borrowing cycle, which in the specific years covered by this essay, was quite vibrant. These years included three international financial crises (Mexico, 1995; Asia, 1997; Russia, 1998) and, within Brazil, were preceded by seven years of hyperinflation and heterodox shocks. There was a monetary reform in 1994; a gigantic deindexation effort and near-crisis in the banking system in 1995 and 1996; the largest privatization program ever between 1993 and 1998 (with assets worth more than US$60 billion sold); and a very aggressive trade-liberalization program that raised import-penetration ratios from 6 percent in 1994 to 20 percent in 1998. This much activity makes it difficult to determine what the optimal choice of an exchange-rate regime should have been and how an equilibrium level for the exchange rate should have been defined.

The issue of currency overvaluation has been part of Real Plan discussions since the very beginning, and interest in it has varied according to the international atmosphere. When markets were buoyant, the issue was left aside; when they were, instead, sluggish, the currency was overvalued by 25 percent or more, or, at least, market participants seemed to consume more intensively the 25 percent overvaluation reports. But apart from market sentiment, which we know is very volatile, there are grounds to support the idea that the currency may strengthen after the end of a hyperinflation, at least as an initial effect of a presumably sound stabilization program (see Sections 3 and 4 above). This may seem more controversial if this new equilibrium is taken as a permanent departure from PPP and is at a point to which exchange rates should always be expected to return, even though, as Kenneth Rogoff says, at a "glacial rate."[60] One must be careful with the

---

[60] "How is it possible to reconcile the extremely high short term volatility of real exchange rates with the glacial rates (15 percent per year) at which deviations from PPP seem to die out?" (Rogoff, 1996, p. 664).

idea that all appreciation must always generate a depreciation of equal size at some point in the future, either through gravity or through the iron rule of PPP.[61] But this is not necessarily the case; it may have been that hyperinflation prompted a long-lasting departure from PPP, an undervaluation that was corrected only with the appreciation brought about by stabilization. As in most hyperinflation cases, it is a question of benchmark. Depending on the choice, there may be no overvaluation at all. *Cosi é se vi pare.*

In spite of all this, it was never denied that some significant appreciation was produced in the early phases of the Real Plan and that some effort was put into reversing it. In the beginning, the gigantic challenge of ending hyperinflation made the need to import stability through the exchange-rate regime seem obvious, especially because one knew that the crucial contribution of fiscal policy in this difficult initial stage was not coming as quickly as it should. In contrast to most cases of exchange-rate-based stabilization, it was the combination of tight money with a float that accomplished the crucial attack on inflation. The ensuing appreciation was, indeed, critical in giving stabilization a strong jump start and in deindexing and dedollarizing the economy in the early stages of the program. It would be very hard to conduct an economy-wide deindexation effort if the indexation of the exchange rate (a crawling peg) were maintained.

It may be fair to reiterate that the Brazilian decision to use a float was not based on doctrine: it was simply the move that best served the stabilization and reform agenda at the time.[62] Not long after, this posture was challenged when, in spite of capital controls at the entry door, sterilized intervention leaning against the wind, and falling interest rates, the exchange rate appreciated to levels that appeared excessive. To prevent further appreciation, it was necessary to define an exchange-rate floor at which the central bank would buy whatever quantity of currency was available. Somewhat later, at the time of the Mexican crisis late in 1994, it became clear that a ceiling as well would

---

[61] In fact, empirical studies tend to show that large appreciations may often, but not always, result in large nominal devaluations (see Goldfajn and Valdés, 1999).

[62] A recent IMF document (1997, p. 24) on the issue of exit from pegged regimes recommends the move toward more flexible regimes "when there are market pressures for appreciation . . . , especially when a country is encountering difficulties contending with large capital inflows." It continues (p. 25), in addition, to assert that "to inaugurate a more flexible exchange rate regime in these circumstances, it is important to announce that the exchange rate will be allowed to move down, as well as up, in response to market forces; and it is important to demonstrate this two-sided flexibility at an early stage."

make sense, so as to avoid a rapid depreciation that would endanger the stabilization process. A full European-style target-zone system was then put into operation *à la Monsieur Jourdan*.

One could have appropriately discussed whether this system delivered less volatility than a float without the edges, or whether it was ideal for a country like Brazil, which, except for brief moments of transition, has been either on the verge of catastrophe or consumed by unrestrained euphoria. More important than theoretical arguments about the best regime, however, was the more mundane issue that the appreciation had gone too far and that, in the presence of the Mexican crisis, capital markets and borrowing prospects had been badly shaken for some time to come. Something had to be done. Some flexibility was necessary to address the new adverse circumstances, but the commitment to stabilization could not be weakened. As a compromise solution, the target zone was moved up in March 1995, producing a nominal devaluation of approximately 8 percent. After that, specific technologies were developed to reduce volatility within the zones and to allow for quiet transitions to higher zones, so that the regime, through time, could prevent further appreciation and allow for some mild devaluation.

The record of bands, as recorded in Figure 6, seems to show that the Brazilian economy has been consistently at the floor, with the central bank calling buy auctions and accumulating reserves, or for briefer moments, at the ceiling, with several sell auctions. This appears to corroborate the notion that Brazil has had no middle ground between crisis and euphoria in these years. After the Mexican crisis and until the Asian crisis, the exchange-rate regime experienced some consolidation. Foreign direct investment recovered strongly, reforms advanced, productivity grew, and inflation fell significantly, from 22 percent in 1995 to 4.3 percent in 1997, as measured by the national CPI (INPC-IBGE), or from 14.8 percent to 7.5 percent, as measured by the IGP-FGV. In 1998, inflation fell to almost zero, and the real-exchange rate recovered by almost 8 percent as a result of the existing crawl.

The decision to be made early in 1999 was whether or not to continue with the gradual devaluation, that is, whether to add another 8 percent to the real exchange rate, with inflation undisturbed at zero, and also whether to widen gradually the existing bands. As argued above, this would have required high interest rates and a somewhat depressed economy for at least a semester. This could seem unbearable to many a politician but, in hindsight, it would not have been a bad course of action. The alternative to a float was not really discussed. Very few people would have dared to speculate about how it would work and what the consequences might be. It is notable that Brazil only allowed the currency to float after an unusual chain of circumstances that began with the failure of the 1997 fiscal package and included the turbulence caused by the Russian moratorium, the lack of political news after President Cardoso's reelection, the president's decision to innovate, and, most important, the failure of the endogenous diagonal band crafted by Dr. Francisco Lopes. The change in Brazil's exchange-rate regime was not an example of prudence and planning.

In the previous section, I argued that a number of crucial policy definitions have yet to be made. When it comes to the exchange-rate regime, or whether Brazil is going to remain with a whole-hearted float, it is useful to inquire, in light of the experience reviewed in this essay, whether there is a third way between the currency board and the pure float (as Bergsten, 1998, proposes). It is useful, in this connection, to quote from a recent IMF document (1997, p. 5) on exit strategies from pegged regimes:

> A policy regime with no firm commitments provides no reliable basis for the formation of expectations and is, therefore, an invitation to instability. . . . The policy regime cannot be the *regime du jour* which is adjusted without constraint to meet the convenience and political exigencies of the moment. Rather, a good and sustainable policy regime must be like a good marriage—for better or worse, for richer or poorer, in good times and bad. The plain fact is that no exchange rate regime and broader economic policy regime is optimal for all countries, or even for a single country, in all circumstances and conditions. A regime must be selected and adhered to on the basis of how it is expected to perform on average in the longer term. Divorce is possible, but it is costly and disruptive—and rightly so.

Commitment is, indeed, a crucial ingredient of any regime, perhaps the more so in the intermediate cases, where there is neither a constitutional obligation to defend the currency nor a legal determination not to intervene. During the last five years, the Brazilian foreign-exchange regime has evolved in ways that are natural in view of the unfolding stabilization and reform agendas, as well as the external circumstances. The regime was tested many times over and never failed to be seen as consistent to the primary policy objectives of the government. The most difficult moments were those in which there were internal divisions in government, as during the first few months of 1995 and the last months of 1998, when government hesitation was clearly seen by markets as a lack of commitment to stay on course, whatever that course was. In such circumstances, speculative attacks might easily have succeeded. When governments hesitate, they are weighing the

81

relative costs of defending the currency and of agreeing to a divorce. This is the time for markets to increase the stakes. In March 1995, the costs of maintaining existing policies were judged to be lower than the costs of departing from them. In January 1999, the decision went the other way, probably as a result of a similar calculation.

The extent of commitment to the exchange-rate regime was always read in Brazil as the willingness to fight for the enabling fundamentals. For this reason, perhaps, the devaluation in 1999 produced a significant loss of credibility, along with an astonishing loss in the president's approval ratings. It will take not only time but a consistent record of promises kept to recover that credibility. There is considerable well-deserved skepticism in the fiscal arena, again the crucial arena for defining the prospects of the Brazilian economy, and the regime change has not helped. It may well be asked whether the choice of an exchange-rate regime can change national agendas to the extent necessary to turn unpopular causes, such as fiscal discipline, into political imperatives. "Too many stabilizations have succumbed," writes Obstfeld (1995, p. 172), "to Sargent-Wallace unpleasant arithmetic because fiscal deficits have continued despite supposedly irrevocable, but ultimately unsustainable, exchange rate targets."

It seems there is an optimal choice between rigidity and flexibility, given the expected pace of correction of fundamentals and the uncertainties along the way. Too much flexibility may imply a lack of commitment and may produce low credibility and instability. Too little, as would occur with a currency board, may be dangerous, because the exit costs, if reforms fail to materialize or experience serious setbacks, will be raised to catastrophic levels. If the road to reforms is long and bumpy, as, indeed, it has been in Brazil, it may be good to have some safeguards and escape clauses. If these are seen as undermining the credibility of such an arrangement,[63] perhaps that arrangement should not be used in the first place. In light of the Brazilian experience, it seems questionable that a very rigid exchange-rate regime will help create *additional* incentives for fiscal discipline. In the presence of an unsustainable fiscal disequilibrium, a currency board is a most certain passport to disaster, and the choice of an exchange-rate regime under such conditions is a second- or third-best choice—or, simply, outright damage control.

The Brazilian trajectory reviewed in this essay may be seen as a series of successive attempts to strike a balance between flexibility and

---

[63] This need not be the case, as is argued on a more abstract level by Cukierman, Kiguel, and Liviatan (1994).

rigidity in view of complex and overlapping domestic agendas, incomplete and uncertain fiscal adjustment, and an unstable international environment. While the fear of returning to hyperinflation was dominant, the emphasis on rigidities prevailed, although they were by no means abused. In fact, the so-called "anchors," most notably, the exchange-rate regime, succeeded ultimately in purging inflation and indexation from the economy. This is an extraordinary gain, but once this accomplishment was made visible, most outstandingly by the remarkably modest inflationary repercussions of the devaluation, flexibility started to enjoy a previously unknown popularity. The loss of an anchor appeared to be acceptable, given the need to be flexible during a time of external turbulence. Besides, nobody seemed comfortable in ruling out another round of extreme instability in Brazil's future, especially if the country lags behind its fiscal obligations, and its southern neighbors experience difficulties. It is hard to argue that a float strengthens the imperative to pursue fiscal discipline. It may be, instead, that the float is the exchange-rate regime that coexists best with fiscal imbalances, at least in the beginning. Brazil may take some time to calculate the effects of crowding-out in an open economy under flexible exchange rates, but it appears that a brand new equilibrium between flexibility and commitments (to the real exchange rate and fiscal policy) will have to be found, most likely within the extremes.

Structural Reforms and Their Impacts

In several passages of this essay, I suggested that the Real Plan, by virtue of the structural reforms it implied, would gradually engineer a transition to a stronger economy. I argued that the economic-development model had to be amended in many ways to fit the new realities of globalization and rapid technological change, not to mention the old anxieties related to economic growth and income distribution. These noble ambitions, and the recollection that several stabilization attempts had failed because they had not addressed the fundamentals, resulted in the Real Plan's being given a mission that was much broader than simply fighting inflation. The concept of reforms rapidly became an all-embracing slogan for a large-scale economic reorientation that would comprise a huge list of large and small items that were often highly specific in their institutional configurations. These involved the private as well as public sector and included all sorts of legal and institutional changes, ranging from constitutional modifications to simple managerial attitudes. Paralleling the old industrial-organization paradigm, structural changes such as stabilization, privatization, and trade liberalization

83

radically transformed economic conduct and, by consequence, brought about significant changes in economic performance. In the private sector, the combination of import competition with the effects of stabilization forced a dramatic turn toward efficiency. In the public sector, the record has been less clear, and there have been questions about the true pace of reforms. Ultimately, the effect of structural (policy) changes (reforms) should be assessed by their impact on economic performance. It is true that the performance of the Brazilian economy improved from 1994 to 1998 in comparison to the previous ten years, especially if we discount the crises in Asia and Russia. But nobody seems satisfied; there is surely potential for much more. Although much has been done to rebuild the basis for economic progress in Brazil, the elements for fast economic growth are not yet all present. Significant obstacles that are still in place are the large fiscal disequilibrium, sectors that are still in need of privatization, inappropriate labor laws, and inefficient spending on education.

Very substantial progress has been made, however, with respect to productivity growth, which directly affects economic expansion. One may argue that, ultimately, reforms are processes through which things can be done progressively better than before, or through which goods and services can be produced at lower costs or with fewer resources. It follows that one indicator of the pace of reforms is growth in productivity. Nothing could better fit the wisdom emerging from modern growth theory, which emphasizes that the roots of sound economic performance should be sought in positive externalities, increasing returns, strategic complementarities, network effects, learning phenomena, and the like. To the extent that productivity growth in Brazil has surpassed past performance, we can argue that, independent of idiosyncratic views on specific actions, reforms are, broadly considered, working, and Brazil is, indeed, building a sound basis for economic growth and competitiveness in the future.

Table 7 shows a summary of studies of productivity growth in Brazil since the early post–World War II period. There are several interesting points to highlight. Note, first, the remarkable performance, in terms of both growth and productivity, from 1950 until the mid–1980s, when there was a marked turn for the worse. During these golden years of increased import substitution, accounting exercises had given a significant role to productivity growth. This should come as a surprise in light of the likely negative association between productivity growth and inward orientation, but it can be explained by the high investment rates, or the capital deepening, that occurred during these

TABLE 7

ESTIMATES OF PRODUCTIVITY GROWTH IN BRAZIL, 1950–1996
(Annual average rates of growth, percent)

Years	Total Factor Productivity Growth		Output Divided by Hours Worked	Gross Domestic Product	
	Elias (1978) and Others	Bonelli and Fonseca (1998)	Bonelli and Fonseca (1998)	Rate of Growth	Per Capita Growth
1950–55	3.8	n.a.	2.7[a]	6.7	3.7
1955–60	3.5	n.a.	2.7[a]	8.2	5.0
1960–65	0.2	3.0[b]	2.5[c]	5.1	2.2
1965–70	2.5	3.0[b]	2.5[c]	7.1	4.0
1971–73	2.1[d]	2.6	5.6	12.4	9.7
1974–80	0.5[e]	–1.0	1.0	7.1	4.5
1981–85	–1.5[f]	–0.4	0.3	1.3	–0.9
1986–90	–1.5[g]	–1.9	–0.8	1.9	0.1
1991–97	n.a.	3.4	7.5[h]	3.1	2.7
Memorandum:					
1970–80	2.6/1.5[i]	n.a.	n.a.	8.8	6.1
1970–84	–0.59	n.a.	n.a.	6.3	3.8

[a] 1949–57.
[b] 1958–70.
[c] 1959–70.
[d] 1970–75.
[e] Hofman and Mulder (1998).
[f] 1980–89; Hofman and Mulder (1998).
[g] 1989–94; Hofman and Mulder (1998)
[h] Moreira (1999).
[i] Pinheiro (1990), estimates for gross output and value-added.
SOURCES: Depec-Banco Central do Brasil; national accounts; and as noted.

years. In the mid–1960s, there was considerable skepticism about the continuation of the growth process once the "easiest part" of import substitution was over. A wave of reforms created the economic miracle of the 1970s, and as a result, in the early 1980s, Brazil was, along with the Asian Tigers, designated as a newly industrialized country, with all the accompanying honors.[64]

---

[64] Moreover, by virtue of its very sound exports performance, Brazil would either be cited as a somewhat curious case of efficient import substitution or placed among outward-oriented countries, thanks to some clever definition of this elusive attribute; see, for example, the World Bank's 1987 *World Development Report* (p. 83).

Brazilian economic performance turned disastrous after 1982. Growth and productivity collapsed, and despite the view that the origins of the problems were external, the lost decade ahead brought a soul-searching debate about the evils produced by excessive protection, regulation, and controls on prices, credit, and investments (see Fritsch and Franco, 1994). Inefficiencies seemed to be widespread, and it was thought (as in the 1960s) that the development model was exhausted and that reforms were needed to expand growth frontiers.

It would seem easy, in this context, to take the evidence of declining productivity growth shown in Table 7 as an expression of the decreasing returns of import substitution, even though a rigorous testing of this assumption would require further research. The positive association between trade orientation and productivity growth seems very clear in the more recent figures, however. This link has been extensively explored in the rather large literature on the subject, so it is hardly surprising that increased openness could have such extraordinary effects on Brazilian manufacturing. Liberalization (along with privatization and deregulation) drastically changed business conduct, exponentially raising interest in themes such as reengineering, downsizing, and total quality control. Nothing of this sort had ever been seen in corporate Brazil.

Meanwhile, FDI penetration increased tremendously the connections of Brazilian industry with global players. Privatizations, as well as mergers and acquisitions involving foreign capital, have occupied a prominent place in recent FDI flows. The entire stock of FDI in Brazil in December 1995 was US$45.5 billion, 55 percent of which was in manufacturing. In 1996, 1997, 1998, and 1999, new inflows of FDI totaled approximately US$83 billion, that is, much more than the existing stock in 1995. Moreover, 70 percent of it went to services and infrastructure.

This new FDI wave will no doubt have large implications for Brazil's trade orientation, as other FDI waves have had in the past.[65] It seems clear, therefore, that something new and very big is happening in

[65] Foreign firms, the shares of which could go as high as 70 percent of manufactured exports, have always been important for Brazilian exports. In addition, foreign firms have been shown to be more export oriented than Brazilian firms with similar attributes, that is, foreign ownership is significantly correlated with export orientation when controlled for other features of the industrial-organization environment. It may therefore be expected that an increase in foreign companies' shares of output in Brazilian manufacturing should increase export orientation. For the historical record and comments on the available evidence, see Fritsch and Franco (1992).

Brazil. Restructuring has been generalized, and its effects on productivity have been equally impressive. There are clear indications that there is a significant change in the productivity growth regime in Brazil, and that its origins should be attributed to reforms. The potential for growth associated with productivity enhancements is thought to be huge (see, for example, the McKinsey Global Institute's 1998 study). A new development model is in the making, with a more open trade orientation, a larger responsibility given to the private sector for investment, and a smaller role given to the state for running the process. We can only hope that macroeconomic instability does not disturb the structural changes set in motion by the reforms that have been part and parcel of the Real Plan.

References

Armijo, Leslie Elliott, "Inflation and Insouciance: The Peculiar Brazilian Game," *Latin American Research Review*, 31 (No. 3, 1996), pp. 7–46.

Bacha, Edmar L., "Moeda, Inércia e Conflito: Reflexões Sobre Política de Estabilização no Brasil," *Pesquisa e Planejamento Econômico*, 18 (April 1988), pp. 1–15.

———, "O Fisco e a Inflação: Uma Interpretação do Caso Brasileiro," *Revista de Economia Política*, 14 (January-March 1994), pp. 5–17.

———, "O Plano Real: Uma Avaliação," in Alosio Mercadante, ed., *O Brasil Pós-Real*, Campinas, São Paulo, Instituto de Economia, Universidade Estadual de Campinas (UNICAMP), 1998, pp. 11–70.

Bergsten, C. Fred, "How to Target Exchange Rates," *Financial Times*, November 20, 1998, p. 24.

Bonelli, Regis, "Growth and Productivity in Brazilian Industries: Impacts of Trade Orientation," *Journal of Development Economics*, 39 (July 1992), pp. 85–109.

Bonelli, Regis, and Renato Fonseca, "Ganhos de Produtividade e Competitividade da Produção Manufatureira no Brasil," Secretaria de Política Econômica (SPE) and Escola Superior de Administração Fazendária (ESAF), Ministry of Finance, Government of Brazil, 1998.

Bruno, Michael, *Crisis, Stabilization, and Economic Reform: Therapy by Consensus*, Oxford, Clarendon, 1993.

Cagan, Phillip, "Hyperinflation," in John Eatwell, Murray Milgate, and Peter Newman, eds., *The New Palgrave: A Dictionary of Economics*, London, Macmillan, 1987.

Calvo, Guillermo A., Leonardo Leiderman, and Carmen M. Reinhart, "Capital Inflows and Real Exchange Rate Appreciation in Latin America," *International Monetary Fund Staff Papers*, 40 (March 1993), pp. 108–151.

Calvo, Guillermo A., and Enrique G. Mendoza, "Petty Crime and Cruel Punishment: Lessons from the Mexican Debacle," *American Economic Review*, 86 (May 1996), Papers and Proceedings, pp. 170–175.

Calvo, Guillermo A., Carmen M. Reinhart, and Carlos A. Végh, "Targeting the Real Exchange Rate: Theory and Evidence," International Monetary Fund Working Paper No. 94/22, Washington, D.C., International Monetary Fund, February 1994.

Cardoso, Eliana, and Ilan Goldfajn, "Capital Flows to Brazil: The Endogeneity of Capital Controls," *International Monetary Fund Staff Papers*, 45 (March 1998), pp. 161–202.

Corbo, Vittorio, and Leonardo Hernández, "Macroeconomic Adjustment to Capital Inflows: Lessons from Recent Latin American and East Asian Experience," *World Bank Research Observer*, 11 (February 1996), pp. 61–85.

Cukierman, Alex, Miguel A. Kiguel, and Nissan Liviatan, "How Much to Commit to an Exchange Rate Rule? Balancing Credibility and Flexibility," in Pierre L. Siklos, ed., *Varieties of Monetary Reforms: Lessons and Experiences on the Road to Monetary Union*, Dordrecht and Boston, Kluwer, 1994, pp. 73–94.

Cunha, Luiz Roberto A., "Congelamento e Políticas Heterodoxas: A Experiência Brasileira," Discussion Paper No. 253, Department of Economics, Pontifícia Universidade Católica do Rio de Janeiro (PUC-RIO), December 1990.

Dornbusch, Rudiger, "Policies to Move from Stabilization to Growth," in *Proceedings of the World Bank Annual Conference on Development Economics 1990*, Washington D.C., World Bank, 1991, pp. 19–48.

———, "Brazil's Incomplete Stabilization and Reform," *Brookings Papers on Economic Activity*, No. 1 (1997), pp. 367–394.

Dornbusch, Rudiger, Ilan Goldfajn, and Rodrigo O. Valdes, "Currency Crises and Collapses," *Brookings Papers on Economic Activity*, No. 2 (1995), pp. 219–270.

Dornbusch, Rudiger, and Mario Henrique Simonsen, "Políticas de Estabilização com Apoio de Políticas de Rendas: Um Exame da Experiência na Argentina, Brasil e Israel," *Revista Brasileira de Economia*, 41 (March 1987), pp. 3–50.

Dornbusch, Rudiger, Federico Sturzenegger, and Holger Wolf, "Extreme Inflation: Dynamics and Stabilization," *Brookings Papers on Economic Activity*, No. 2 (1990), pp. 1–64.

Edwards, Sebastian, "Latin America's Underperformance," *Foreign Affairs*, 76 (March-April 1997), pp. 93–103.

———, *Real Exchange Rates, Devaluation and Adjustment: Exchange Rate Policies in Developing Countries*, Cambridge, Mass., MIT Press, 1989.

Eichengreen, Barry, and Albert Fishlow, "Contending with Capital Flows: What Is Different about the 1990s?" in Miles Kahler, ed., *Capital Flows and Financial Crises*, New York, Council of Foreign Relations, Cornell University Press, 1998, pp. 23–68.

Eichengreen, Barry, Donald Mathieson, Bankim Chadha, Anne Jansen, Laura Kodres, and Sunil Sharma, *Hedge Funds and Financial Market Dynamics*, Occasional Paper No. 166, Washington, D.C., International Monetary Fund, May 1998.

Elias, Victor Jorge, "Sources of Economic Growth in Latin American Countries" *Review of Economics and Statistics*, 6 (August 1978), pp. 362–370.

Ferretti, Gian Maria, and Assaf Razin, *Current-Account Sustainability*, Princeton Studies in International Finance No. 81, Princeton, N.J., Princeton University, International Finance Section, October 1996.

Fishlow, Albert, "Is the Real Plan for Real?" in Susan K. Purcell and Riordan Roett, eds., *Brazil under Cardoso*, Boulder, Colo., Lynne Rienner, 1997, pp. 43–62.

————, "Indexing Brazilian Style: Inflation without Tears?" *Brookings Papers on Economic Activity*, No. 1 (1974), pp. 261–280.

Folkerts-Landau, David, "Derivatives: The New Frontier in Finance," in Tomás J. T. Baliño and Carlo Cottarelli, eds., *Frameworks for Monetary Stability: Policy Issues and Country Experiences*, Washington, D.C., International Monetary Fund, IMF Institute, and Monetary and Exchange Affairs Department, 1994.

Franco, Gustavo H. B., *O Plano Real e Outros Ensaios*, Rio de Janeiro, Francisco Alves, 1995.

Fritsch, Winston, and Gustavo H. B. Franco, "Foreign Direct Investment and Patterns of Industrialization and Trade in Developing Countries: The Brazilian Experience," in Gerald K. Helleiner, ed., *Trade Policy, Industrialization and Development*, Oxford, Clarendon, 1992.

————, *The Political Economy of Trade and Industrial Policy Reform in Brazil in the 1990s*, Santiago, United Nations Economic Commission for Latin America and the Caribbean, 1993.

————, "Import Compression, Productivity Slowdown and Manufactured Exports Dynamism: Brazil, 1975–90," in Gerald K. Helleiner, ed., *Trade Policy and Industrialization in Turbulent Times*, London, Routledge, 1994, pp. 63–95.

Garcia, Marcio G. P., and Alexandre Barcinski, "Capital Flows to Brazil in the 1990s: Macroeconomic Aspects and the Effectiveness of Capital Controls," *Quarterly Review of Economics and Finance*, 38 (Fall 1998), pp. 319–357.

Goldberg, Pinelopi K., and Michael M. Knetter, "Goods Prices and Exchange Rates: What Have We Learned?" *Journal of Economic Literature*, 35 (September 1997), pp. 1243–1272.

Goldfajn, Ilan, and Rodrigo O. Valdés, "The Aftermath of Appreciations," *Quarterly Journal of Economics*, 114 (February 1999), pp. 229–262.

Guimarães, Eduardo A., Henry Pourchet, and Ricardo A. Markwald, "Índices de Rentabilidade das Exportações Brasileiras," Discussion Paper No. 130, Fundação Centro de Estudos de Comércio Exterior (Funcex), July 1997.

Guitián, Manuel, "Exchange Rate Management in the Reform Process," in Richard C. Barth, Alan R. Roe, and Chong-Huey Wong, eds., *Coordinating Stabilization and Structural Reform*, Proceedings of a Seminar, Washington, D.C., IMF Institute, 1993.

Hofman, André A., and Nanno Mulder, "The Comparative Productivity Performance of Brazil and Mexico," in John H. Coatsworth and Alan M. Taylor, eds., *Latin America and the World Economy Since 1800*, Cambridge, Mass., Harvard University Press, 1998, pp. 85–110.

International Monetary Fund (IMF), "Exit Strategies: Policy Options for Countries Seeking Greater Exchange Rate Flexibility," Washington, D.C., International Monetary Fund, Research Department, in consultation with the Monetary and Exchange Affairs Department and the Policy Development and Review Department, December 1997.

Jochum, Christian, and Laura Kodres, "Does the Introduction of Futures on Emerging Market Currencies Destabilize the Underlying Currencies?" International Monetary Fund Working Paper No. 98/13, Washington, D.C., International Monetary Fund, February 1998.

Krueger, Anne, "Foreign Trade Regimes and Economic Development: Liberalization Attempts and Consequences," Cambridge, Mass., National Bureau of Economic Research, processed 1978.

Krugman, Paul, "Dutch Tulips and Emerging Markets," *Foreign Affairs*, 74 (July-August 1995), pp. 28–44.

———, "The Myth of Asia's Miracle," in *Pop Internationalism*, Cambridge, Mass., and London, MIT Press, 1996, pp. 167–187.

Lall, Subhir, "Speculative Attacks, Forward Market Intervention and Classic Bear Squeeze," International Fund Working Paper 97/164, Washington, D.C., International Monetary Fund, December 1997.

Lee, Jang-Yung, "Implications of a Surge in Capital Inflows: Available Tools and Consequences for the Conduct of Monetary Policy," International Fund Working Paper 96/53, Washington, D.C., International Monetary Fund, May 1996.

McKinsey Global Institute, *Productivity—the Key to an Accelerated Development Path for Brazil*, São Paulo and Washington, D.C., McKinsey Global Institute, 1998.

Mann, Frederick A., *The Legal Aspect of Money, with Special Reference to Comparative Private and Public International Law*, 5th edition, Oxford, New York, Toronto, and Melbourne, Clarendon, 1992.

Modigliani, Franco, and Tommaso Padoa-Schioppa, *The Management of an Open Economy with "100% Plus" Wage Indexation*, Essays in International Finance No. 130, Princeton, N.J., Princeton University, International Finance Section, December 1978.

Moreira, Maurico Mesquita, "Abertura Comercial e Indústria: Atualizando os Resultados," Technical Note, Rio de Janeiro, Banco Nacional de Desenvolvimento Econômico e Social (BNDES), 1997.

Obstfeld, Maurice, "International Currency Experience: New Lessons and Lessons Relearned," *Brookings Papers on Economic Activity*, No. 1 (1995), pp. 119–196.

90

Pinheiro, Armando Castelar, "Measuring and Explaining Total Factor Productivity Growth: Brazilian Manufacturing in the 1970s," Discussion Paper No. 189, Rio de Janeiro, Instituto de Pesquisa Econômica Aplicada (IPEA), March 1990.

Polak, Jacques J., "The Articles of Agreement of the IMF and the Liberalization of Capital Movements," in Stanley Fischer, Richard N. Cooper, Rudiger Dornbusch, Peter M. Garber, Carlos Massad, Jacques J. Polak, Dani Rodrik, and Savak S, Tarapore, *Should the IMF Pursue Capital-Account Convertibility?* Essays in International Finance No. 207, Princeton, N.J., Princeton University, International Finance Section, May 1998.

Rebelo, Sergio, and Carlos A. Végh, "Real Effects of Exchange-Rate-Based Stabilization: An Analysis of Competing Theories," in Ben S. Bernanke and Julio J. Rotemberg, eds., *NBER Macroeconomics Annual 1995*, Cambridge, Mass., and London, MIT Press, 1995.

Reinhart, Carmen M., and R. Todd Smith, "Too Much of a Good Thing: The Macroeconomic Effect of Taxing Capital Inflows," Washington, D.C., International Monetary Fund and University of Maryland, March 1997, processed.

Rodrik, Dani, "The Limits of Trade Policy Reform in Developing Countries," *Journal of Economic Perspectives*, 6 (Winter 1992), pp. 87–106.

Rogoff, Kenneth, "The Purchasing Power Parity Puzzle," *Journal of Economic Literature*, 34 (June 1996), pp. 647–668.

Roldós, Jorge E., "Supply-Side Effects of Disinflation Programs," *International Monetary Fund Staff Papers*, 42 (March 1995), pp. 158–183.

Salm, Claudio, Joao Saboia, and Paulo Gonzaga M. de Carvalho, "Produtividade na Indústria Brasileira: Questões Metodológicas e Novas Evidências Empíricas" (with English summary), *Pesquisa e Planejamento Econômico*, 27 (August 1997), pp. 377–396.

Shapiro, Matthew D., and David W. Wilcox, "Mismeasurement in the Consumer Price Index: An Evaluation," in Ben S. Bernanke and Julio J. Rotemberg, eds., *NBER Macroeconomics Annual 1996*, Cambridge, Mass., and London, MIT Press, 1996, pp. 93–142.

Thomas, Vinod, and John Nash, with Sebastian Edwards and others, *Best Practices in Trade Policy Reform*, Oxford, New York, Toronto, and Melbourne, Oxford University Press for the World Bank, 1991.

Williamson, John, "Crawling Bands or Monitoring Bands: How to Manage Exchange Rates in a World of Capital Mobility," *International Economics Policy Briefs*, No. 99–3, Washington, D.C., World Bank, February 1999.

World Bank, *Brazil: An Agenda for Stabilization*, Report No. 13168–BR, Washington, D.C., World Bank, 1994.

United Nations Conference on Trade and Development (UNCTAD), *World Investment Report 1997: Transnational Corporations, Market Structure and Competition Policy*, Geneva, United Nations, 1997.

PUBLICATIONS OF THE
INTERNATIONAL FINANCE SECTION

Notice to Contributors

The International Finance Section publishes papers in four series: ESSAYS IN INTERNATIONAL FINANCE, PRINCETON STUDIES IN INTERNATIONAL FINANCE, and SPECIAL PAPERS IN INTERNATIONAL ECONOMICS contain new work not published elsewhere. REPRINTS IN INTERNATIONAL FINANCE reproduce journal articles previously published by Princeton faculty members associated with the Section. The Section welcomes the submission of manuscripts for publication under the following guidelines:

ESSAYS are meant to disseminate new views about international financial matters and should be accessible to well-informed nonspecialists as well as to professional economists. Technical terms, tables, and charts should be used sparingly; mathematics should be avoided.

STUDIES are devoted to new research on international finance, with preference given to empirical work. They should be comparable in originality and technical proficiency to papers published in leading economic journals. They should be of medium length, longer than a journal article but shorter than a book.

SPECIAL PAPERS are surveys of research on particular topics and should be suitable for use in undergraduate courses. They may be concerned with international trade as well as international finance. They should also be of medium length.

Manuscripts should be submitted in triplicate, typed single sided and double spaced throughout on 8½ by 11 white bond paper. Publication can be expedited if manuscripts are computer keyboarded in WordPerfect or a compatible program. Additional instructions and a style guide are available from the Section.

How to Obtain Publications

The Section's publications are distributed free of charge to college, university, and public libraries and to nongovernmental, nonprofit research institutions. Eligible institutions may ask to be placed on the Section's permanent mailing list.

Individuals and institutions not qualifying for free distribution may receive all publications for the calendar year for a subscription fee of $45.00. Late subscribers will receive all back issues for the year during which they subscribe.

Publications may be ordered individually, with payment made in advance. ESSAYS and REPRINTS cost $10.00 each; STUDIES and SPECIAL PAPERS cost $13.50. An additional $1.50 should be sent for postage and handling within the United States, Canada, and Mexico; $1.75 should be added for surface delivery outside the region.

All payments must be made in U.S. dollars. Subscription fees and charges for single issues will be waived for organizations and individuals in countries where foreign-exchange regulations prohibit dollar payments.

Information about the Section and its publishing program is available at the Section's website at www.princeton.edu/~ifs. A subscription and order form is printed at the end of this volume. Correspondence should be addressed to:

International Finance Section
Department of Economics, Fisher Hall
Princeton University
Princeton, New Jersey 08544-1021
Tel: 609-258-4048 • Fax: 609-258-6419
E-mail: ifs@princeton.edu

List of Recent Publications

A complete list of publications is available at the International Finance Section website at www.princeton.edu/~ifs.

ESSAYS IN INTERNATIONAL FINANCE

178. Alberto Giovannini, *The Transition to European Monetary Union*. (November 1990)
179. Michael L. Mussa, *Exchange Rates in Theory and in Reality*. (December 1990)
180. Warren L. Coats, Jr., Reinhard W. Furstenberg, and Peter Isard, *The SDR System and the Issue of Resource Transfers*. (December 1990)
181. George S. Tavlas, *On the International Use of Currencies: The Case of the Deutsche Mark*. (March 1991)
182. Tommaso Padoa-Schioppa, ed., with Michael Emerson, Kumiharu Shigehara, and Richard Portes, *Europe After 1992: Three Essays*. (May 1991)
183. Michael Bruno, *High Inflation and the Nominal Anchors of an Open Economy*. (June 1991)
184. Jacques J. Polak, *The Changing Nature of IMF Conditionality*. (September 1991)
185. Ethan B. Kapstein, *Supervising International Banks: Origins and Implications of the Basle Accord*. (December 1991)
186. Alessandro Giustiniani, Francesco Papadia, and Daniela Porciani, *Growth and Catch-Up in Central and Eastern Europe: Macroeconomic Effects on Western Countries*. (April 1992)
187. Michele Fratianni, Jürgen von Hagen, and Christopher Waller, *The Maastricht Way to EMU*. (June 1992)
188. Pierre-Richard Agénor, *Parallel Currency Markets in Developing Countries: Theory, Evidence, and Policy Implications*. (November 1992)
189. Beatriz Armendariz de Aghion and John Williamson, *The G-7's Joint-and-Several Blunder*. (April 1993)
190. Paul Krugman, *What Do We Need to Know About the International Monetary System?* (July 1993)
191. Peter M. Garber and Michael G. Spencer, *The Dissolution of the Austro-Hungarian Empire: Lessons for Currency Reform*. (February 1994)
192. Raymond F. Mikesell, *The Bretton Woods Debates: A Memoir*. (March 1994)
193. Graham Bird, *Economic Assistance to Low-Income Countries: Should the Link be Resurrected?* (July 1994)
194. Lorenzo Bini-Smaghi, Tommaso Padoa-Schioppa, and Francesco Papadia, *The Transition to EMU in the Maastricht Treaty*. (November 1994)
195. Ariel Buira, *Reflections on the International Monetary System*. (January 1995)
196. Shinji Takagi, *From Recipient to Donor: Japan's Official Aid Flows, 1945 to 1990 and Beyond*. (March 1995)
197. Patrick Conway, *Currency Proliferation: The Monetary Legacy of the Soviet Union*. (June 1995)
198. Barry Eichengreen, *A More Perfect Union? The Logic of Economic Integration*. (June 1996)
199. Peter B. Kenen, ed., with John Arrowsmith, Paul De Grauwe, Charles A. E.

Goodhart, Daniel Gros, Luigi Spaventa, and Niels Thygesen, *Making EMU Happen—Problems and Proposals: A Symposium.* (August 1996)
200. Peter B. Kenen, ed., with Lawrence H. Summers, William R. Cline, Barry Eichengreen, Richard Portes, Arminio Fraga, and Morris Goldstein, *From Halifax to Lyons: What Has Been Done about Crisis Management?* (October 1996)
201. Louis W. Pauly, *The League of Nations and the Foreshadowing of the International Monetary Fund.* (December 1996)
202. Harold James, *Monetary and Fiscal Unification in Nineteenth-Century Germany: What Can Kohl Learn from Bismarck?* (March 1997)
203. Andrew Crockett, *The Theory and Practice of Financial Stability.* (April 1997)
204. Benjamin J. Cohen, *The Financial Support Fund of the OECD: A Failed Initiative.* (June 1997)
205. Robert N. McCauley, *The Euro and the Dollar.* (November 1997)
206. Thomas Laubach and Adam S. Posen, *Disciplined Discretion: Monetary Targeting in Germany and Switzerland.* (December 1997)
207. Stanley Fischer, Richard N. Cooper, Rudiger Dornbusch, Peter M. Garber, Carlos Massad, Jacques J. Polak, Dani Rodrik, and Savak S. Tarapore, *Should the IMF Pursue Capital-Account Convertibility?* (May 1998)
208. Charles P. Kindleberger, *Economic and Financial Crises and Transformations in Sixteenth-Century Europe.* (June 1998)
209. Maurice Obstfeld, *EMU: Ready or Not?* (July 1998)
210. Wilfred Ethier, *The International Commercial System.* (September 1998)
211. John Williamson and Molly Mahar, *A Survey of Financial Liberalization.* (November 1998)
212. Ariel Buira, *An Alternative Approach to Financial Crises.* (February 1999)
213. Barry Eichengreen, Paul Masson, Miguel Savastano, and Sunil Sharma, *Transition Strategies and Nominal Anchors on the Road to Greater Exchange-Rate Flexibility.* (April 1999)
214. Curzio Giannini, *"Enemy of None but a Common Friend of All"? An International Perspective on the Lender-of-Last-Resort Function.* (June 1999)
215. Jeffrey A. Frankel, *No Single Currency Regime Is Right for All Countries or at All Times.* (August 1999)
216. Jacques J. Polak, *Streamlining the Financial Structure of the International Monetary Fund.* (September 1999)
217. Gustavo H. B. Franco, *The Real Plan and the Exchange Rate.* (April 2000)

PRINCETON STUDIES IN INTERNATIONAL FINANCE

68. Mark Gersovitz and Christina H. Paxson, *The Economies of Africa and the Prices of Their Exports.* (October 1990)
69. Felipe Larraín and Andrés Velasco, *Can Swaps Solve the Debt Crisis? Lessons from the Chilean Experience.* (November 1990)
70. Kaushik Basu, *The International Debt Problem, Credit Rationing and Loan Pushing: Theory and Experience.* (October 1991)
71. Daniel Gros and Alfred Steinherr, *Economic Reform in the Soviet Union: Pas de Deux between Disintegration and Macroeconomic Destabilization.* (November 1991)

72. George M. von Furstenberg and Joseph P. Daniels, *Economic Summit Declarations, 1975-1989: Examining the Written Record of International Cooperation.* (February 1992)
73. Ishac Diwan and Dani Rodrik, *External Debt, Adjustment, and Burden Sharing: A Unified Framework.* (November 1992)
74. Barry Eichengreen, *Should the Maastricht Treaty Be Saved?* (December 1992)
75. Adam Klug, *The German Buybacks, 1932-1939: A Cure for Overhang?* (November 1993)
76. Tamim Bayoumi and Barry Eichengreen, *One Money or Many? Analyzing the Prospects for Monetary Unification in Various Parts of the World.* (September 1994)
77. Edward E. Leamer, *The Heckscher-Ohlin Model in Theory and Practice.* (February 1995)
78. Thorvaldur Gylfason, *The Macroeconomics of European Agriculture.* (May 1995)
79. Angus S. Deaton and Ronald I. Miller, *International Commodity Prices, Macroeconomic Performance, and Politics in Sub-Saharan Africa.* (December 1995)
80. Chander Kant, *Foreign Direct Investment and Capital Flight.* (April 1996)
81. Gian Maria Milesi-Ferretti and Assaf Razin, *Current-Account Sustainability.* (October 1996)
82. Pierre-Richard Agénor, *Capital-Market Imperfections and the Macroeconomic Dynamics of Small Indebted Economies.* (June 1997)
83. Michael Bowe and James W. Dean, *Has the Market Solved the Sovereign-Debt Crisis?* (August 1997)
84. Willem H. Buiter, Giancarlo M. Corsetti, and Paolo A. Pesenti, *Interpreting the ERM Crisis: Country-Specific and Systemic Issues.* (March 1998)
85. Holger C. Wolf, *Transition Strategies: Choices and Outcomes.* (June 1999)
86. Alessandro Prati and Garry J. Schinasi, *Financial Stability in European Economic and Monetary Union.* (August 1999)

SPECIAL PAPERS IN INTERNATIONAL ECONOMICS

16. Elhanan Helpman, *Monopolistic Competition in Trade Theory.* (June 1990)
17. Richard Pomfret, *International Trade Policy with Imperfect Competition.* (August 1992)
18. Hali J. Edison, *The Effectiveness of Central-Bank Intervention: A Survey of the Literature After 1982.* (July 1993)
19. Sylvester W.C. Eijffinger and Jakob De Haan, *The Political Economy of Central-Bank Independence.* (May 1996)
20. Olivier Jeanne, *Currency Crises: A Perspective on Recent Theoretical Developments.* (March 2000)

REPRINTS IN INTERNATIONAL FINANCE

28. Peter B. Kenen, *Ways to Reform Exchange-Rate Arrangements*; reprinted from *Bretton Woods: Looking to the Future*, 1994. (November 1994)
29. Peter B. Kenen, *Sorting Out Some EMU Issues*; reprinted from Jean Monnet Chair Paper 38, Robert Schuman Centre, European University Institute, 1996. (December 1996)

○ SUBSCRIBE ○ ORDER ○

INTERNATIONAL FINANCE SECTION

SUBSCRIPTIONS

Rate $45 a year

The International Finance Section issues six to eight publications each year in a mix of Essays, Studies, and occasional Special Papers and Reprints. Late subscribers receive all publications for the subscription year. Prepayment is required and may be made by check in U.S. dollars or by Visa or Master-Card. A complete list of publications is available at www.princeton.edu/~ifs.

Address inquiries to:

International Finance Section
Department of Economics, Fisher Hall
Princeton University
Princeton, NJ 08544–1021

BOOK ORDERS

Essays & Reprints	$10.00
Studies & Special Papers	$13.50

plus postage

Within U.S.	$1.50
Outside U.S. (surface mail)	$1.75

_____

Discounts are available for book dealers and for orders of five or more publications.

_____

Telephone: 609–258–4048
Telefax: 609–258–6419
E-mail: ifs@princeton.edu

fold up

INTERNATIONAL FINANCE SECTION

This is a subscription ☐ ; a book order ☐

Essay #(s) _____, _____ No. of copies___

Study #(s) _____, _____ No. of copies___

Special Paper # _____   No. of copies ___

Reprint # _____   No. of copies ___

☐ Enclosed is my check made payable to Princeton University, International Finance Section

totaling $_____.

Please charge: ☐ Visa ☐ MasterCard

Acct.# _____

Expires _____

Signature_____

Send to:

Name_____

Address_____

City _____

State _____Zip _____

Country_____

INTERNATIONAL FINANCE SECTION
DEPARTMENT OF ECONOMICS
FISHER HALL
PRINCETON UNIVERSITY
PRINCETON, NJ 08544-1021

The work of the International Finance Section is supported
in part by the income of the Walker Foundation, established
in memory of James Theodore Walker, Class of 1927. The
offices of the Section, in Fisher Hall, were provided by a
generous grant from Merrill Lynch & Company.

ISBN 0-88165-124-9